LOS ANGELES

Lost And Found

Essays on Identity, Place, and Belonging

MARGARET CHANDRA KERRISON

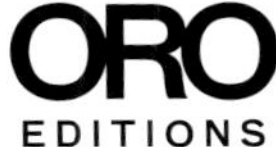
EDITIONS

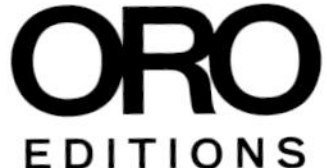

Publishers of Architecture, Art, and Design
Gordon Goff: Publisher

www.oroeditions.com
info@oroeditions.com

Published by ORO Editions

Author: Margaret Chandra Kerrison
ORO Managing Editor: Jake Anderson
Layout Design, Illustrations & Book Cover: Yamuna & Bhagwat, Chaitanya Agency (www.wearechaitanya.com)

10 9 8 7 6 5 4 3 2 1 First Edition

ISBN: 978-1-966515-43-2

Color Separations and Printing: ORO Editions, Inc.
Printed in China.

International Distribution: www.oroeditions.com/distribution

ORO Editions makes a continuous effort to minimize the overall carbon footprint of its publications. As part of this goal, ORO Editions, in association with Global ReLeaf, arranges to plant trees to replace those used in the manufacturing of the paper produced for its books. Global ReLeaf is an international campaign run by American Forests, one of the world's oldest nonprofit conservation organizations. Global ReLeaf is American Forests' education and action program that helps individuals, organizations, agencies, and corporations improve the local and global environment by planting and caring for trees.

LOS ANGELES
Lost And Found

Essays on Identity, Place, and Belonging

MARGARET CHANDRA KERRISON

Contents

Dedication

To the people of Los Angeles, and
to those who carry her spark.

“Tip the world over on its side and everything loose will land in Los Angeles.”

Frank Lloyd Wright

“And because we were
in Southern California—in
Hollywood even—there was
no history for us. There were
no books or traditions telling
us how we could turn out or
what anything meant.”

Eve Babitz

Foreword

When Margaret messaged me she was writing this collection of essays about Los Angeles and the stories it holds, it made complete sense.

In the years I've known her, I've watched her grow into one of the world's foremost immersive storytellers, shaped in no small part by the creative energy of her adopted home, Los Angeles.

In the same message, she asked me to write the foreword to this book, which a year ago I would have balked at because I am but a face in this metropolis of millions. But, after an extremely challenging year for all of us in LA, I recognize the city has become part of my story too.

Unlike Margaret, LA was never a place I thought I would end up, let alone call home.

Sure, LA was where all of my relatives had settled after emigrating from Taiwan. I'd see my California cousins on summer breaks, their deeply tanned legs peeping from their basketball shorts from days spent outdoors when, I imagined, they weren't stuck in their cars. After living most of my life up and down the Eastern seaboard, I envisioned settling down somewhere quieter, low-key and certainly with more cloud cover.

But years later I found myself in LA. Work and family proved to be a unifying, gravitational force.

I came to LA to report for a public radio station covering the city's many diasporas. It's where I got married on a warm October day in Chinatown and, years later, had two kids—one born in Pasadena, the other in Hollywood.

My husband and I bought our first home in LA's San Gabriel Valley, a tiny post-World War II boxy house in the foothill community of Altadena. Behind our narrow, sloped lot rose the majestic San Gabriels. And from the front porch, if you stood in the right spot, you could glimpse the twinkle of downtown LA in the far distance through our neighbors' trees.

Altadena embodied everything beautiful and singular about LA. Nature trails threaded the foothills, mere minutes from the rush of the 210 freeway. The community also reflected a kind of diversity that felt special in a city defined by racial and economic boundaries. On our block alone, families came from a range of racial and cultural backgrounds. The Black homeownership rate of 81% was nearly double the national average. Our neighbors were accountants, artists, educators, and touring musicians.

As I write about Altadena, I'm realizing that I'm using the past tense and the conditional and that it's because we're not living there at the moment. On January 7, 2025, the Eaton Fire tore through half our community, taking our home and virtually every house on our street.

This year's wildfires have unmoored tens of thousands of us across LA. For our family, what had been our little hideaway amid the city's hum and hustle became rubble and ash overnight, heaved onto dump trucks for parts unknown.

We are now renting in a town thirty-five-minutes south, although our lives still orbit around Altadena for school, playdates, and Little League.

All this tumult has brought into question: *What is home?* Is it our old house, lost along with all the totems of our lives, from childhood photo albums to our daughter's favorite quilt?

Or is home what we hold inside, like the bonds to our dear neighbors now scattered and to those friends who rallied near and wrapped us in love and care?

More and more I think it's the latter. Paradoxically, the fires actually drew us closer to LA—not just to the place itself, but to the community it holds.

Margaret's deeply reflective and optimistic essays underscore this collective spirit of LA, while paying tribute to the individuals who make this city every day. They come as the city grapples with the aftermath of the fires and now the immigration raids on our fellow Angelenos that have made so many streets and neighborhoods go silent.

The city desperately needs hope right now, and Margaret's observations about LA's past show how upheaval can also be a catalyst for positive change. Los Angeles, she reminds us, is a living, breathing place built by dreamers those who persist. In doing so, she offers us something we could use right now: a vision of LA not only as it is and was, but what it can be.

— Josie Huang, public radio journalist for LAist

Introduction

When the LA wildfires struck earlier this year in 2025, every single Angeleno was affected. Many of us lost homes, businesses, schools—places of community. Places that defined who we are, both as individuals and as a collective. Even for those of us who didn't lose these physical spaces, the impact rippled through us. We felt the pain of our friends, neighbors, and fellow Angelenos. We grieved with them in ways we had never experienced before. Because this wildfire—this level of devastation—had not been seen in recent memory. It was a disaster that struck at the heart, shook us to the core, and forced us to question what truly matters.

We came together as a city-state. We poured our hearts into the communities of Altadena and Pacific Palisades—through donations, volunteering, and emotional support. We stood side by side in the streets of LA. We understood, deeply, that this could have happened to any one of us, depending on where the wind blew.

During this time, I began writing essays—initially as personal reflections on the wildfires and what it means to rebuild. I approached it through my lens as an experience and environmental designer. I wondered: how do you pick up the pieces—whatever's left—and start again? How do you tell a story not just of loss, but of community, resilience, and love?

Over time, these essays became love letters to Los Angeles. A city that has given me so much. A city that welcomed me as I was—and continues to welcome me as I evolve. I remembered what brought me here in the first place, how I've grown alongside a city that is constantly reimagining and reinventing itself. A place I've chosen to call home for the past twenty-one years, alongside my husband and son. This is the only home my twelve-year-old has ever known. He is a true product of the many cities we've lived in across Greater LA area.

My hope is that, by reading these essays, you feel a deep resonance—and a reminder of why this city is so extraordinary. LA is a city of contradictions. For all its beauty and flaws, its spirit exists only here.

It's where I've been both lost and found. And where I continue to be—because this city doesn't judge. It accepts you as you are, with your strengths and your flaws. Just like itself. It welcomes those who dare to dream, to take risks, to grow, and above all—to remain incomplete.

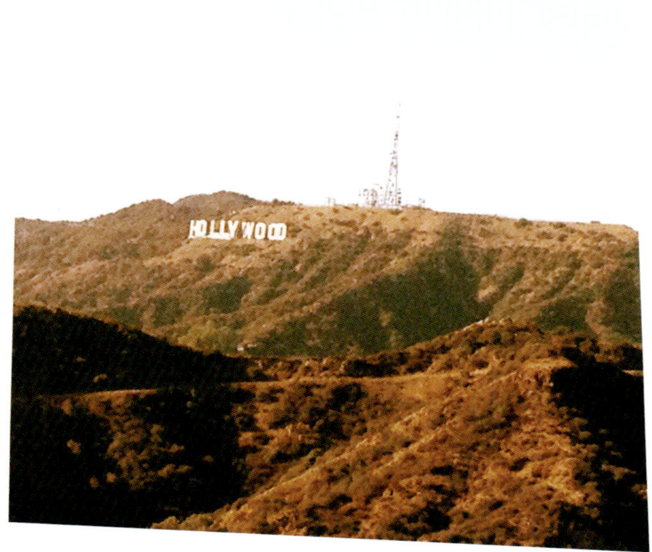

Hollywood sign.
Photo by Margaret Kerrison

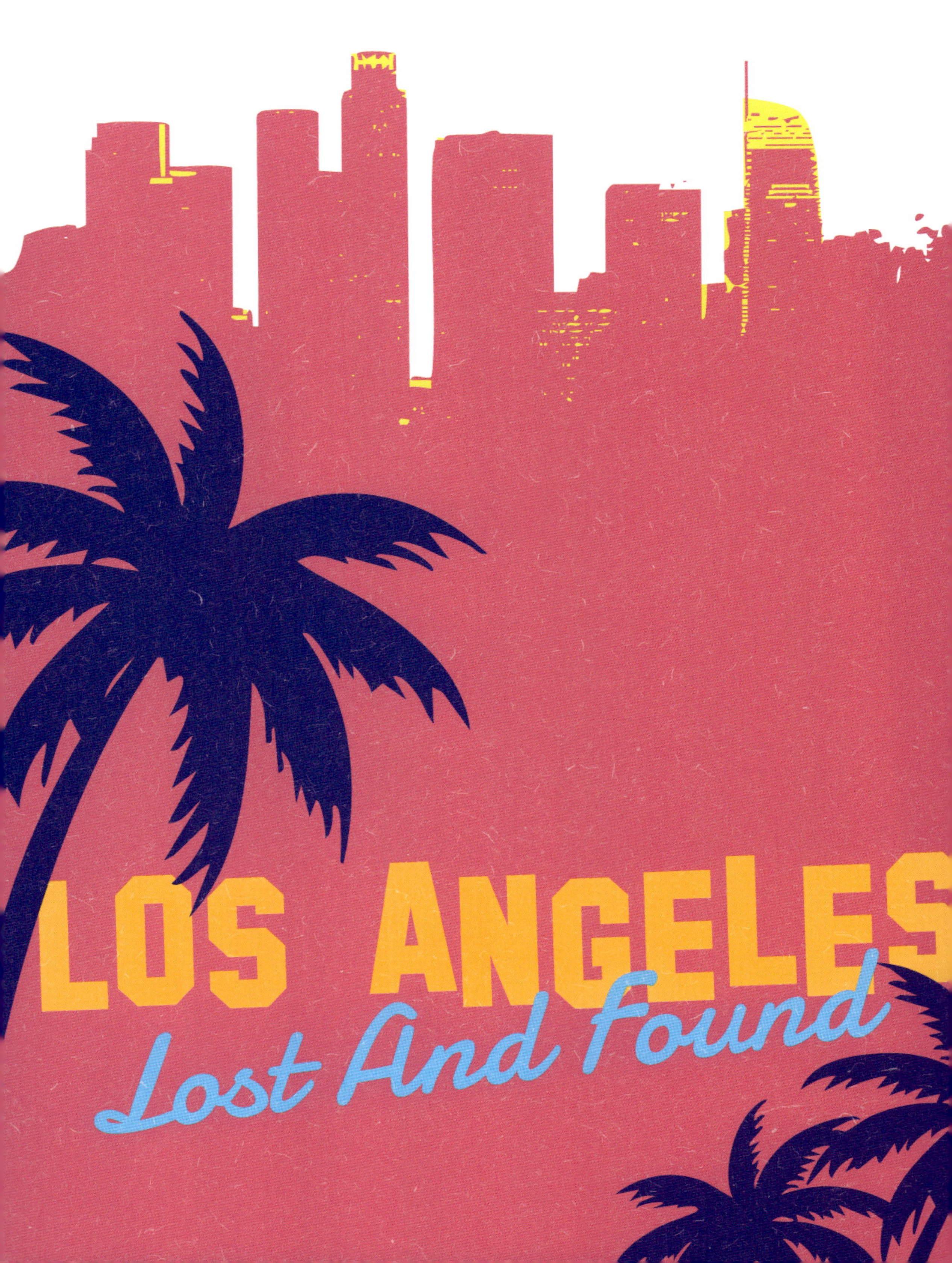
LOS ANGELES
Lost And Found

Los Angeles has been called many things: the City of Angels, the City of Dreams, La-La Land, and Hollyweird. Each name reflects a different part of its identity. But the nickname "Lost Angeles" has always struck a chord with me, perhaps due to its subtle irony. To some, it symbolizes a loss of identity or disillusionment with the entertainment industry. To me, it represents a place where people can lose themselves, reinvent, and emerge anew.

This metaphor feels more poignant than ever in the aftermath of the devastating wildfires. The physical manifestation of "Lost Angeles" has forced us all to pause, confront our realities, and envision a new way forward. The fires created a ripple effect deeply tied to this city—a collective reckoning that shook us. They prompted reflection on what was, what is, what we've lost, and what we might still create. The fires reminded us of life's impermanence: everything, everywhere, and everyone are fleeting moments and memories.

So how do we live in the present while looking toward the future, honoring the past without being bound by it? How do we rebuild this city with purpose, understanding what is truly meaningful, usable, and essential? Perhaps, in losing, we've gained the clarity to reimagine what Los Angeles—and life—can be.

I personally know friends who lost their homes in Altadena, along with the countless pieces of their lives they held. For one family, it began with a power outage, forcing them to flee in the middle of the night, with not much more than the clothes on their backs. They thought they would return in a couple of nights, like many who evacuated their homes. In the flames, they lost their daughter's cherished electric keyboard, their son's favorite books and toys, and so much more. A house is more than just walls—it's a vessel for memories, a sanctuary for the physical tokens of a family's journey. What do you do when it all disappears? And what does it mean for something to be "lost" when it wasn't misplaced, but taken by forces beyond one's control? Or perhaps it was misplaced—our meaning, security, and comfort—hidden in objects we never realized anchored us to a sense of stability. How do you say goodbye to the things that defined your life?

This reckoning with change and impermanence reminds all of us Angelenos that this city, like life itself, is always in a state of evolving

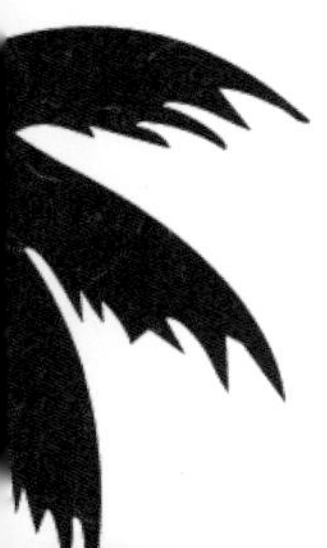

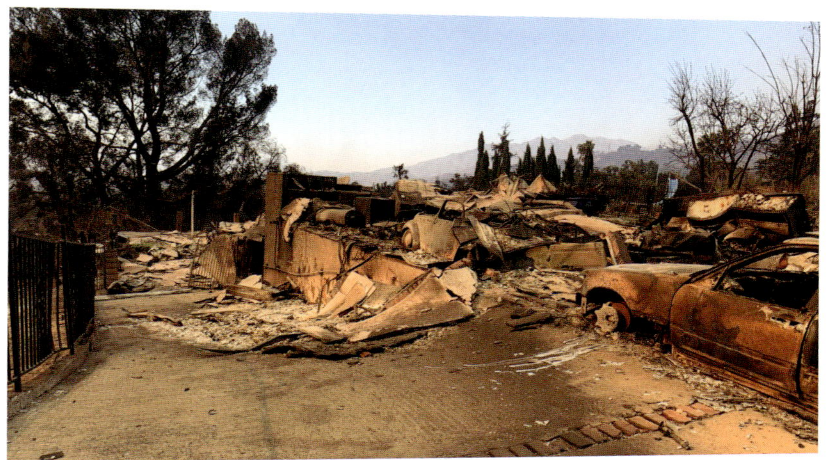

Image obtained through a public records request from the State of California, originally published via DINS 2025 Eaton Public View[1]. Uploaded using Wikimedia Commons UploadWizard. Author unspecified

and becoming. Rebuilding after devastation is as intrinsic to Los Angeles as its rush hours. Wildfires are woven into this region's natural cycles, yet this one was particularly vast, devastating, and impacted so many densely populated communities.

When people think of wildfires in Los Angeles, they often think of Malibu or the Pacific Palisades—places where celebrity homes are lost, garnering media attention and public empathy. But Altadena is different. Its faces may be unfamiliar to many, yet they are everywhere—teachers, nurses, small business owners, grocery store workers, and restaurant staff. They are the people we encounter daily in schools, hospitals, places of worship, markets, and streets. They aren't figures from our screens, but from our real, shared lives.

Altadena's community reflects the heart of this city: immigrants, working-class families, and minorities who have built Los Angeles's backbone. They prepare meals for our children, clean the offices we leave behind, and keep our neighborhoods running. Many chose Altadena for the promise of homeownership, finding in it one of the few affordable paths to stability in this sprawling, expensive city. These were families with dreams—not just for themselves but for their loved ones, hoping to pass down their homes to future generations. They sought more than houses—they sought the opportunity to build lives filled with purpose and promise. Multiple generations of the same families lived side by side, fostering a tight-knit community that would be challenging, if not impossible, to replicate.

Now, those dreams lie in ashes. Unlike wealthier areas, they didn't have the resources to hire private firefighting crews or the luxury of comprehensive fire insurance. For some, rebuilding to what they had is simply out of reach. For others, it may feel like an impossibility. In facing this loss, it may seem like the end—of homes, security, and the futures they envisioned. Yet, as with so many who have come to this city, they will have to decide how to rise again.

For those with greater fortune, this devastation marks a new beginning—a chance to recover and rebuild, replacing what was lost with something that may not be identical but will come close. With resources, insurance, and support networks, they will rise from the ashes, reconstructing homes and lives. For some, it may even

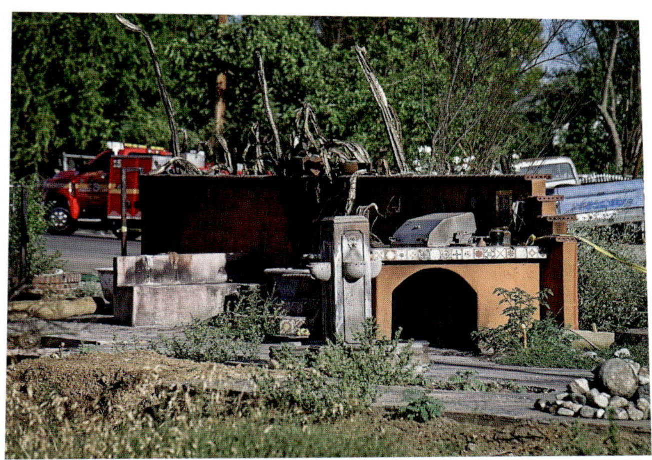

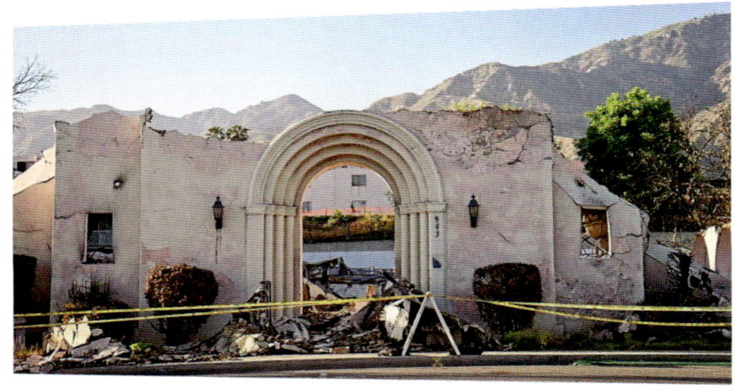

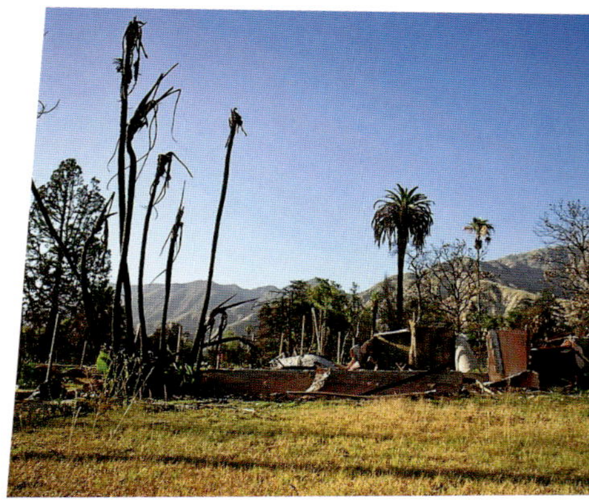

Six months after wildfires tore through
Altadena, CA, the devastation remains.
An entire community lost.
Photos by Foster Kerrison

become an opportunity to reimagine their futures in ways they never dared before.

Take the owner of a bookstore in Pasadena. He lost his home in the fires, yet when his store reopened, the community flooded in to offer support. I learned of his story not through the news, but via Instagram. These raw, unpolished stories resonated deeply because they felt real—relatable in a way that made us pause and think, "That could've been me." If the wind had shifted direction, if the flames had spread to Griffith Park instead of Eaton Canyon, it could have been my family fleeing into the night, my home reduced to embers. I asked myself the same questions those affected must face: What would I have saved? Where would I go? Would I rebuild here or start somewhere else?

I visited the bookstore the first weekend it reopened. I saw John sitting behind his desk in his usual spot, conducting business as if nothing had happened—as though he hadn't just lost his home or faced the possibility of losing his store. I had never spoken to him before, but his presence always reassured me. It reminded me that there are people in my community who share the same love I do: a passion for the written word.

I was relieved to see him there, pricing newly donated books. At one point, I overheard him on the phone telling a concerned customer that he was doing okay, staying in an Airbnb while sorting things out. Like the person on the other end of the call, I too felt relief. My support, however, wasn't in words of comfort but through my purchase of books. That was my contribution. Everyone has their own way of giving.

When I think about the impact of these wildfires, it's not the COVID pandemic that comes to mind—it's the feeling I had after 9/11 when I was a grad student in Boston. I frequently visited friends in New York City. It wasn't just fear of the unknown—it was the presence of a tangible threat, the enemy had a face, and we didn't know where they would strike next. I can't fully imagine what New York endured during that time, as the ripple effects were felt globally. The wildfires, by contrast, aren't a global event. Their impact is intensely localized, affecting the people here in Los Angeles who have built their lives in this city.

Two decades ago, I came here with my husband to reinvent myself. I left my job at a software company in Boston to pursue my dream of becoming a writer. I enrolled in USC's School of Cinematic Arts for an MFA in screenwriting, hoping to write the next great American movie or binge-worthy series. Instead, I found a different dream.

Los Angeles helped me not only redefine myself but also discover a dream uniquely mine. I found the world of themed entertainment, where I could create and design immersive experiences in museums, theme parks, and beyond. I fell in love with world-building—reimagining places that don't yet exist. As many in LA now face the challenge of reimagining and rebuilding their worlds, this idea feels especially relevant.

As a first-generation immigrant, Los Angeles was where I chose to start a family. Since I was eleven, I've been drawn to this city, enchanted by Hollywood movie studios, Rodeo Drive, and Disneyland. When people ask where I'm from, I answer, "Born in Indonesia, raised in Singapore, made in LA." This city helped me find my identity and my path. This city is a reflection of who you are and who you want to be. It holds a mirror up to your face, allowing you to reimagine yourself. There's space here for every version of you, and you can change as many times as

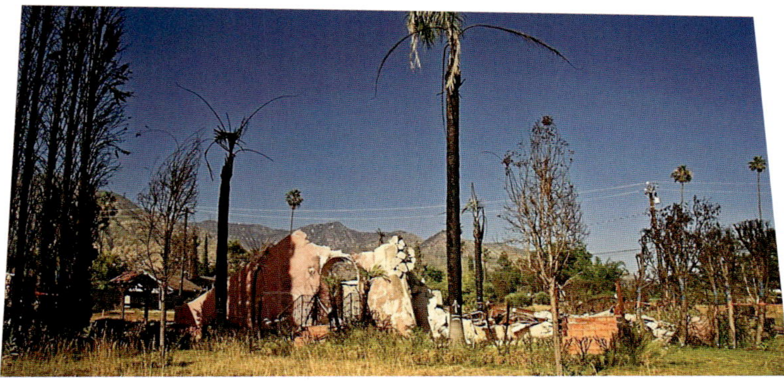

The remains of a once-beloved home. Photo by Foster Kerrison

you want. No one will judge you. Many of us stay busy—constantly moving, changing, and adapting. When asked, "How are you?" the answer is usually, "Busy," and that's how we like it. The state is busy, productive, a place for doers as much as dreamers.

Los Angeles has always been a place for those wanting to make something of themselves. People here roll up their sleeves and get to work. From its early days as orange groves and desert, this city has evolved into a place where builders and planners reshape it to meet the needs of the present. Los Angeles is a place not afraid of reinvention—constantly transforming, constantly adapting. It's a city of experimentation.

But that constant change can make it difficult to find a sense of identity or belonging. Los Angeles is always in flux; the only constant is change. For those who embrace it, this city is a perfect fit. It's a land of improbabilities, filled with people who refuse to take "no" for an answer. It's a city where possibilities are endless, but if you can't open your mind to new opportunities, there's little space for you. For those who can, this city is yours.

For those who have made Los Angeles their home, we accept that this city is improbable. It's not naturally suited for humans to live in this climate. It's dry and prone to drought, with long stretches of scorching heat and limited water resources. The region sits atop multiple fault lines, making it vulnerable to devastating earthquakes. It faces seasonal wildfires that threaten homes and landscapes. The natural environment doesn't easily support large populations or sprawling urban development.

Yet, despite these challenges, millions have chosen to make LA their home. They've adapted through innovation, resilience, and sheer determination—creating vast infrastructure to bring water from hundreds of miles away, developing building codes to withstand natural disasters, and forging a vibrant culture that embraces diversity and reinvention.

In many ways, LA's existence is a testament to human perseverance and ingenuity—a city that thrives not because nature made it easy,

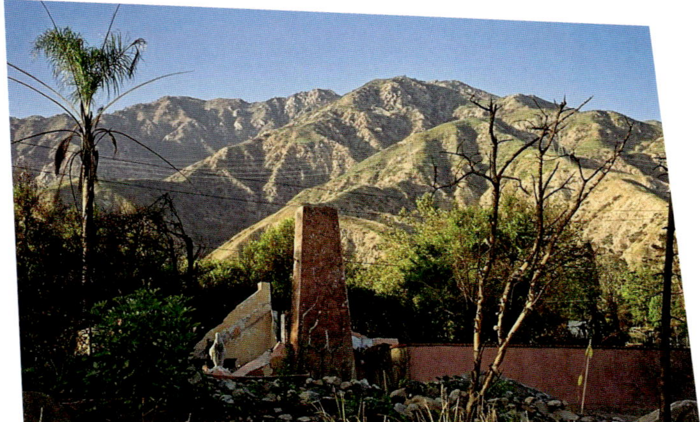

A chimney is all that remains of this former home in Altadena, CA. Photo by Foster Kerrison

but because people refused to be stopped by obstacles. We learn to coexist with nature.

We understand from our shared history that we must rebuild and design structures that can withstand wildfires, earthquakes, and the broader impacts of the climate crisis. These challenges are everywhere, but how we rebuild now can serve as a model for other cities. The world is watching, and we can all learn from one another's experiences.

Despite being a sprawling metropolis divided by freeways and area codes, Los Angeles is an interconnected web of communities. We take pride in our neighborhoods, each with its own identity. We don't choose where we live just for convenience—we choose places that reflect who we are. Our neighborhoods aren't just where we live; they're where we find belonging.

We Angelenos all know someone affected by the fires—a coworker, a neighbor, a friend. This shared experience has united us in a way I haven't seen in my two decades here. For the first time, the city feels united in vulnerability. It could have been me, but it was you. And because it was you, I can imagine what you're going through. Your unfamiliar face feels achingly familiar because, in another version of this story, it was my face.

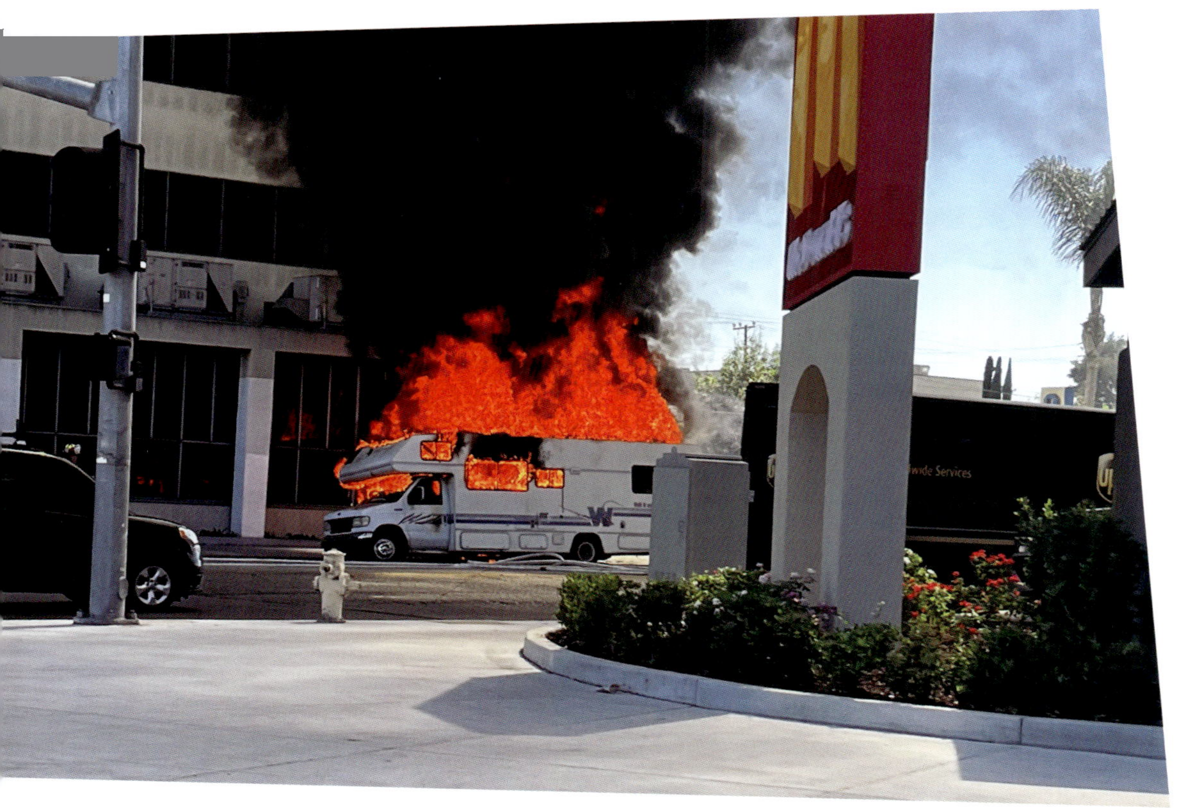

RV on fire, North Hollywood, CA.
Photo by Bryce Kerrison

WHAT WE DIDN'T LOSE *In The Fire*

I imagine what we've lost in the fire. During the recent wildfires, my family faced the unsettling act of packing for an evacuation. While Burbank was spared from the flames, the emotional impact lingers. As we packed a week's worth of clothes, we had to decide what we couldn't bear to lose. Alongside essentials like passports, laptops, and birth certificates, I carefully chose items that carried emotional weight—my jewelry, gifts from my grandmother who is no longer with us, and pieces from my mother, given during happier times. These are more than objects; they are memories I treasure.

I calmly told our eleven-year-old son that he could pack one duffle bag full of what he wanted to keep. He filled it with books and a Soot Sprite keychain from *Spirited Away*, that his Yima, my sister, gave him. He packed his iPad and Nintendo Switch, his most prized possessions.

I looked around the house and paid close attention to all the "things" we own. As someone who identifies as an essentialist, I feel detached from most possessions. Like anyone, I enjoy acquiring something new now and then, but I rarely form strong attachments to objects. I let go of things easily—perhaps too easily. My husband and son are always complaining that I donate or discard items too often, too soon. Compared to a typical middle-aged woman, I don't own much in the way of clothes, shoes, or accessories. My most valued possessions are my passport, phone, and laptop; I can't imagine life without them.

Over the past few weeks, I've envisioned all my belongings consumed by flames. Oddly, I feel a strange sense of liberation. Our home, while modestly filled, sometimes overwhelms me with its objects. Walking from room to room, I realize most of what surrounds me is not truly mine. Aside from the essentials, everything else feels replaceable. I only have a handful of things from my childhood. Most of the things I owned from growing up in Singapore were thrown away when my father sold our childhood home. My husband, by contrast, packed many sentimental items, including family photo albums, preserving memories from the days of film photography.

In my social feeds, I see families whose lives have been devastated by the fires. Their fundamental needs—shelter and safety—are gone. All their belongings reduced to ashes. It makes me reflect on how much we value our possessions and the critical role they play in shaping

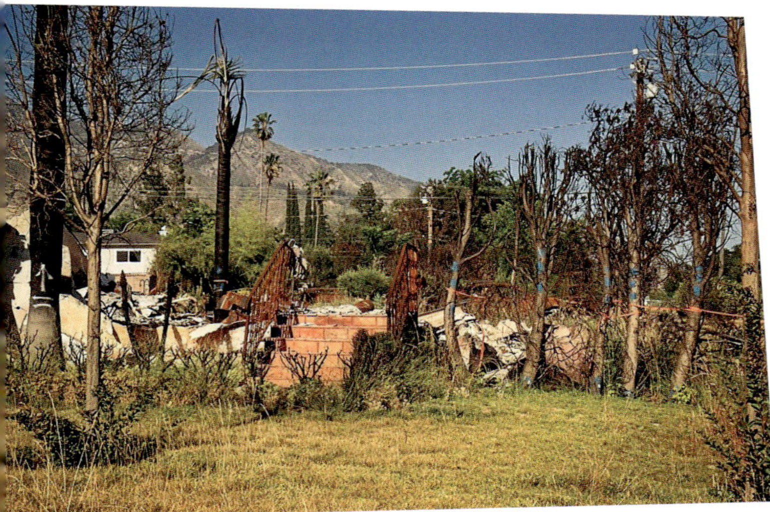

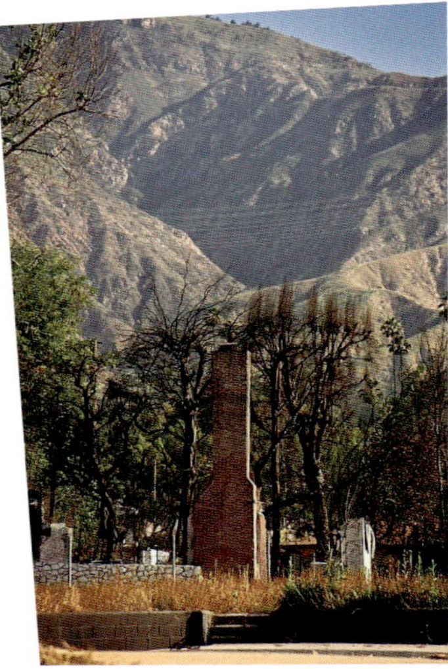

Families evacuated with barely any time to gather belongings.
Photos by Foster Kerrison

our identities. These objects become anchors for our sense of self and memory. They serve as powerful reminders of the lives we've lived—trophies and treasures, testaments to the memories we hope to preserve.

As humans, we are constantly trying to understand who we are and who we are becoming. Often, we look to the past for clues. The things we surround ourselves with serve as tangible markers of that identity. Our homes, in turn, become shrines of memory, repositories of our unique journeys, and reflections of the people we've shared them with. They become personal narratives, a kind of placemaking. It makes me wonder, how do we mark a place as ours? By our things, of course. By the things we keep and leave behind. They represent who we are or perhaps who we want to be.

A beloved house filled with vintage furniture is not so different from a park adorned with locally made art. Both reflect the tastes, values, and stories of the individuals or communities that create them. These objects aren't merely decorative—they are symbols of history and identity. In this sense, placemaking isn't just about constructing physical spaces; it's about curating meaningful collections that resonate emotionally.

I think of a small yellow vase I treasure. I bought it in a ceramic shop my sister and I stumbled upon while wandering through the streets of Lisbon. The vase isn't particularly beautiful, but it encapsulates a memory. The store, housed in what used to be an antique watch shop, had charming little shelves and drawers. The young shopkeeper's warmth made us feel like friends, not tourists. Though the shop no longer exists, the memory lives on in that vase. Every time I look at it or touch it, it's like a time machine that brings me back to that moment in Lisbon.

A vase holds a story, just as a town square with murals or statues tells a community's story. Similarly, in our homes, heirlooms and cherished decor transform a space into something more than functional. They are vessels of memory, connecting us to the past and giving us a sense of belonging.

I also have a cherished batik cloth that hangs in my bedroom. It's one of the first things I see when I wake and one of the last I see before sleep. It holds a memory of my last trip to Indonesia with my grandmother, shortly before she passed away from COVID-19. We bought it at a small stall while driving back from Madura Island, near my birthplace, Surabaya. I remember the young shopkeeper, a mother, tending the store as her baby played in the dirt. My mother and I shared a moment watching that child. Now, when I see the batik, I think of motherhood—my grandmother, my mother, myself, and that young mother. This is the power of some of our things: they become portals, transporting us back to moments we cherish.

Our relationship with things—objects, possessions, and the material traces of our lives—shapes not only our spaces but also our sense of self. These items aren't just belongings; they're vessels for story. They speak to where we've been, what we value, and who we hope to become. In the spaces we call home, in the corners of public parks or the walls of community centers, objects become anchors for memory and identity.

This is the essence of placemaking: the art of creating spaces that carry meaning, that reflect the lives and values of the people who inhabit them. It's not just about design or aesthetics—it's about storytelling. And stories, unlike trends, endure.

When I scroll through my social feeds and see families that have lost everything in wildfires—homes reduced to ash, photos turned to dust—I'm struck by the emotional gravity of objects. Not because they are expensive, but because they hold memory. A mug passed down from a grandmother. A child's drawing pinned to the fridge. A well-worn armchair in the corner of the room. These are the quiet artifacts of our lives, infused with meaning, irreplaceable not for their utility, but for their emotional weight.

I often wonder: What would it look like to build our spaces around the stories that matter most to us? To treat our belongings not as décor, but as chapters of our personal histories?

Today, though, it often feels like placemaking has been overtaken by aesthetics. We see spaces curated for social media—designed for the shares, meant to impress rather than express. Public plazas feature costly installations by famous artists instead of showcasing local talent. Homes are styled for Instagram perfection. Shops are arranged like movie sets. These places might dazzle, but they rarely linger in memory. They invite admiration, not belonging.

Yet I find that the most meaningful places are rarely the most polished. A community garden where neighbors swap tomatoes and stories. A living room with mismatched furniture but a warmth you can feel. A local coffee shop bulletin board layered with handwritten notes. These are spaces that live and breathe because they reflect real people, not trends.

The tension between spectacle and authenticity is real. And in placemaking, it matters. Because while designers can sketch a vision, only the community can decide whether a space becomes part of their story. This is why early, honest conversations are so vital. When people are invited into the design process—when they're asked: What do you need? What do you love? What do you remember?—

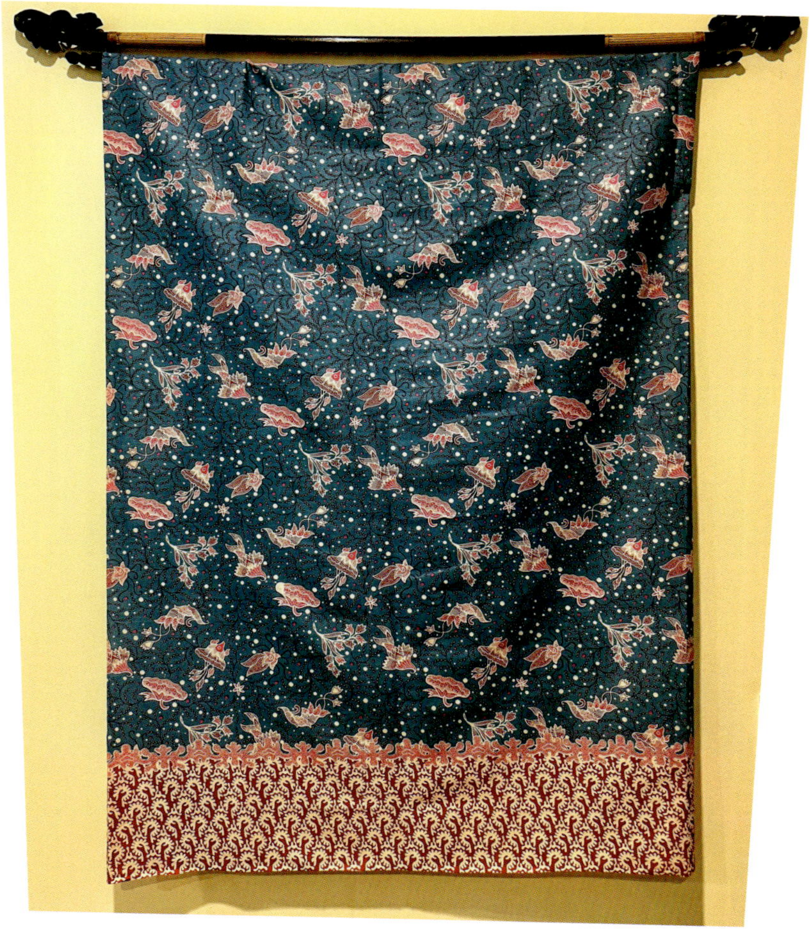

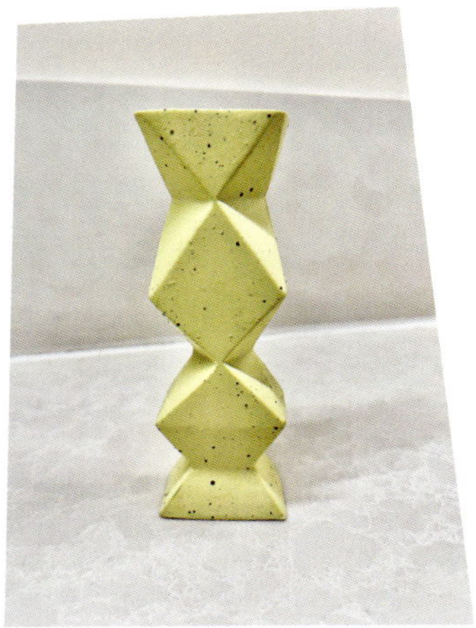

Batik cloth from Madura, Indonesia.
Vase from Lisbon, Portugal.
Photos by Margaret Kerrison

the result is more than just a functional space. It becomes a shared creation, imbued with meaning.

I envision a future where communities gather not just to rebuild after loss, but to reimagine together. Where the scars left by fire, flood, or time are honored. Where objects lost are mourned, and new ones are chosen with care. Symbols of resilience. Artifacts of hope. Vessels for new memories.

Imagine, in the reconstruction of Altadena, a space where the community can embed pieces found in the ashes of their homes—fragments set into the cement floor like mosaic tiles, forming a walkway that takes everyone on a journey through the things they treasured and lost. Picture this walkway beginning with pieces of memory and culminating in a beautiful courtyard with a water fountain—a refuge, a hopeful place where one can sit on a bench, surrounded by serenity and filled with a sense of hope and community.

Imagine a community center at the heart of the greatest devastation. This community center would be more than just a building—it would be

The aftermath of Christmas morning at home in Burbank, CA.
Photo by Margaret Kerrison

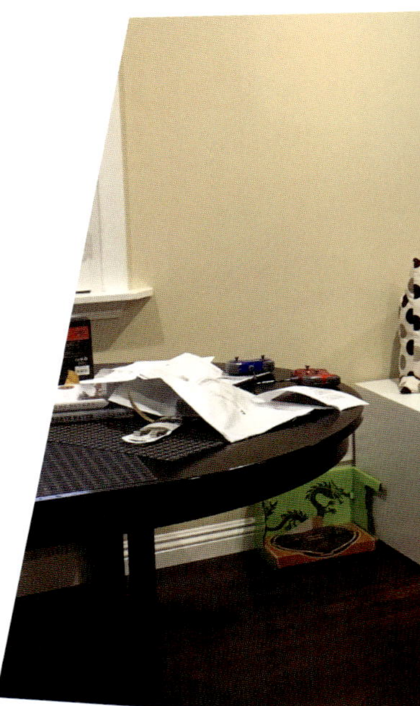

a gathering place where people come not only to share their stories, but to listen, reflect, and rebuild together. It would host workshops, memory circles, and art projects that invite people of all ages to process loss and celebrate resilience. Walls could display photos, drawings, and words from those who lived through the fire, creating a living exhibit of shared experience. In this space, storytelling becomes a form of rebuilding—a foundation laid not with bricks alone, but with empathy, remembrance, and collective strength.

Because, when everything falls away, what remains is what always mattered: the people, the stories, and the values that hold us together. Whether it's a charred photograph we manage to salvage or the piece of fabric from a curtain, these are the pieces we carry forward. They become part of a larger, ongoing narrative—a bridge between what was and what can be.

True placemaking begins here: not with objects, but with meaning. With the stories we choose to tell, and the spaces we create to hold them.

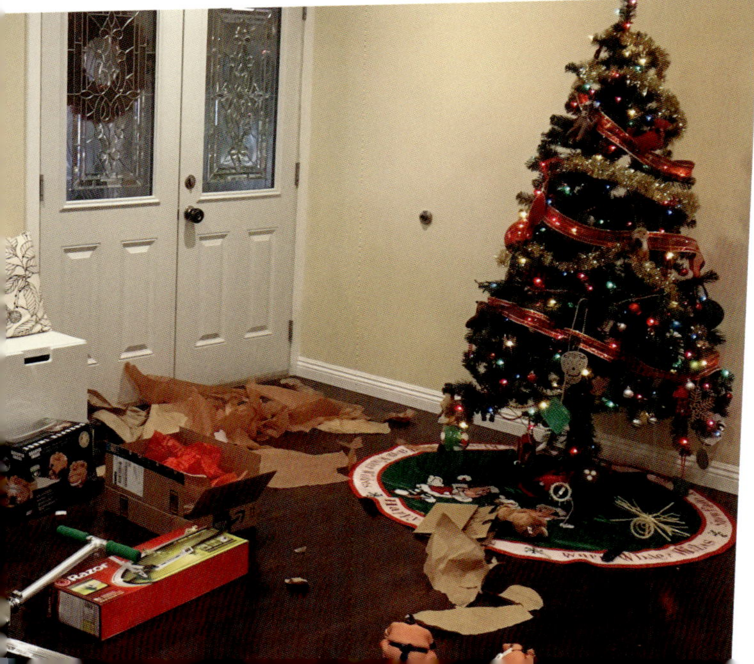

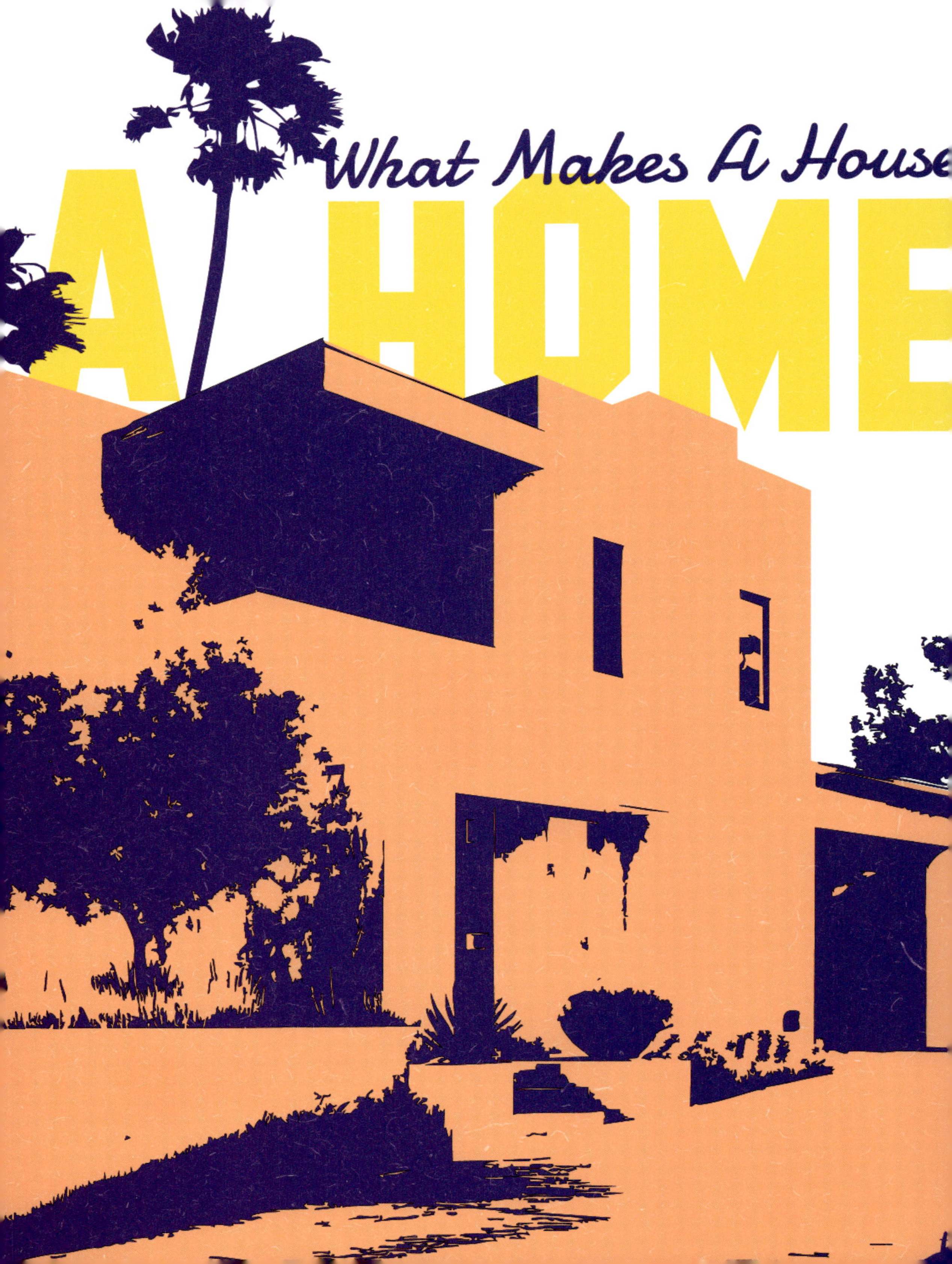
What Makes A House
A HOME

I remember the feeling of stepping through our front door, greeted by my beloved dog—a Papillon with big ears and an even bigger personality. I remember the sound the mailbox made when my aunt took out the mail. That sound—small, mundane—meant I was home from school. It meant dinner would soon fill the air with familiar scents like *mee goreng* or steamed fish with black bean sauce. This was home for most of my childhood.

It was the home where I played with Barbies, filmed skits with my sister and friends on the family camcorder, hosted birthday parties and sleepovers, and navigated both calculus homework and my parents' divorce. It was where I introduced my first boyfriend, dressed up for prom, and later got ready for high school graduation.

We returned for many summers, but it never felt quite the same. My aunt moved back to Surabaya, and eventually, my dad sold the house. Just like that, it slipped out of our lives—no longer ours, no longer home.

It wasn't my first home, but it's the one I remember most vividly—filled with memories, hopes, and dreams. In the first three years of my life, I lived in two different houses in Surabaya before relocating to Singapore. I don't remember the first one at all. The second was so large it frightened me. I imagined ghosts lurking in every corner, especially in the dark, mostly unused second floor, where one side held my parents' bedroom. I dreaded going upstairs at night.

In my first eighteen years, I moved across continents, time zones, and cultures. What is home when the walls around you keep changing? When ceilings shift in color and height, when the air carries unfamiliar scents, when the floors no longer recognize your footsteps, and the voices around you no longer feel like your own?

I've moved more times than I can count. Starting with my biggest move—from Singapore to Boston for college—and then moving every year to a new dorm or apartment. At first, it was a novelty. It was fun to think of each year as a new chapter, dreaming about where I'd live and how I'd arrange my space. I reimagined what my life could be every time I moved. But each move, I realize now, came with a cost.

Every time I displaced myself, I lost a part of myself—and began a new story.

Displacement isn't just about geography—it's about losing the anchor of familiarity, and being thrown into unfamiliar spaces where you must restart. When you're constantly uprooting yourself, you leave behind a life you've known—rebuilding toward another one. This constant shifting unmoors you in ways that are deeply unsettling.

How many uprootings can we endure before they begin to fracture our sense of self—our community, our identity, our sense of belonging, and security? Is it routine and consistency that make a home, or something else entirely?

Dislocation is emotional archaeology. In every relocation, you are both the excavator and the buried artifact—digging through layers of yourself to salvage what still feels like you. You arrive with boxes, sometimes. But more often, you arrive with nothing more than the people you love and the memories that survive the move.

In that raw, stripped-down moment, you begin to understand something essential: a house is a structure; a home is a story. It's what you carry with you when everything else is left behind—the smell of a familiar dish, the echo of a loved one's voice, the stories you choose to remember and retell. And slowly, piece by piece, you start building again—not just a new life, but a new version of yourself.

And I, as an environmental designer and experiential storyteller, believe that we are the narrators of that story. Even if there are no familiar photos on the walls, no mementos from our travels on the shelves, we carry the spirit of our stories with us: the songs we sing to our children, the rituals we perform each morning, the inside jokes passed between family members across a dinner table.

You can create home without your belongings You can build it with laughter and stories. With the music you carry with you—even in a borrowed home. With the shared memory of who you are together, not where you are.

I've walked through luxury model homes, pristine and polished, but cold—soulless. And I've also sat on bare floors in tiny apartments, surrounded by unpacked boxes and takeout containers, and felt more at home than anywhere else. Why? Because a house becomes a home only when we infuse it with presence, purpose, possibility, and love. Without that—without us—a house is just an address.

When is a house not a home?
When you can't see yourself in it.
When you cannot be vulnerable in it.
When you are merely surviving within it—not belonging to it.
When you can't experience joy in it.

I think often of my grandmother's last house in Surabaya—the many summers we spent there playing ping pong and cards. The house she passed away in, lying on her bed. The bed where she used to massage our feet and tell epic stories—how she met our grandfather, stories of us as children, tales woven with love, care, and drama.

Our family no longer owns the house my grandma, my *emak,* lived in, but the structure is still there. It lives on in the stories we tell—in the way I display mementos from the years I spent visiting her, in the way I hang photos on my wall—even now, continents away. That house is gone. But that home? It's still here. It's in me. Every house I've ever lived in, I carry with me.

In the end, perhaps home is not a place at all.

Perhaps it's a feeling—a fleeting, fragile moment we build again and again with the people we love, in the spaces we choose to root ourselves in, even temporarily. Home is not about permanence. It's about presence.

So wherever you are—even if you feel lost, even if the familiar has been stripped away—look to the people beside you. The stories you carry. The rituals you refuse to let go of.

You are home.
When you bring it with you.

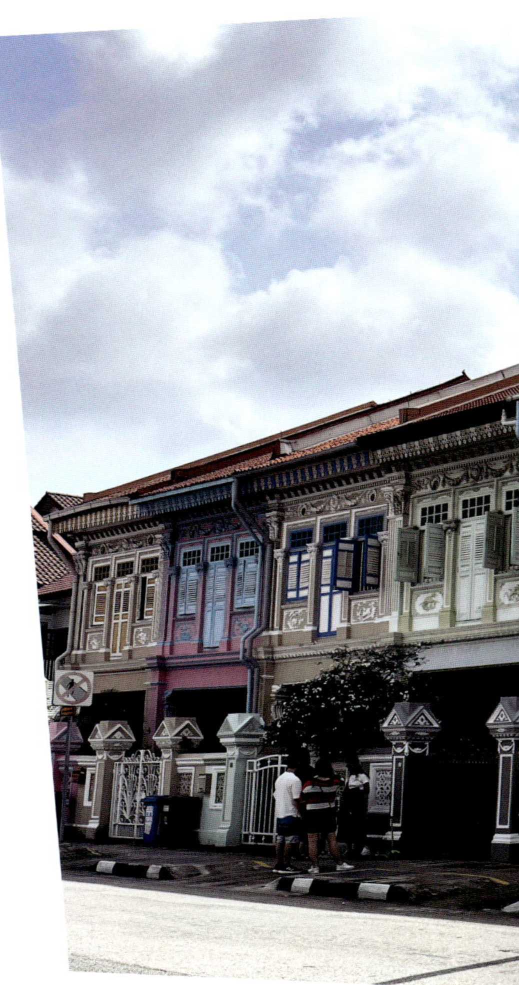

Classic Singaporean shophouses—narrow and typically two to three stories tall—traditionally featuring a ground-floor shop with living quarters above. Photo by Margaret Kerrison

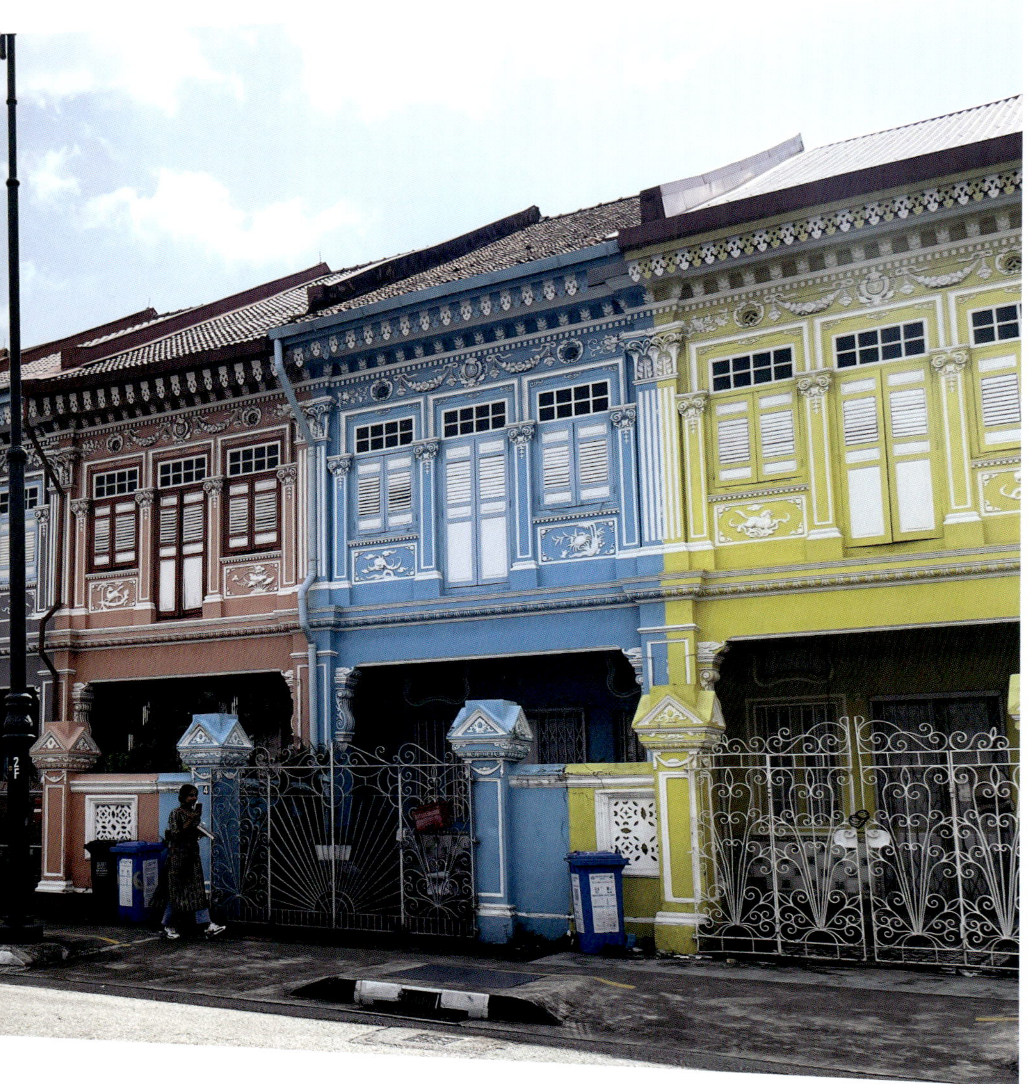

In EMAK'S Room

This is the room I return to often in my memory—the room where I see her. My *emak*, my grandma, sitting beside me on the flowered bedsheets of her king-size bed, reading the local newspaper, talking on the phone, watching television. The sound of her dogs barking in the garage. The smell of *Baygon* sprayed every evening to rid the room of mosquitoes before we prepared for sleep. How we had to evacuate the room for at least an hour to let the smell dissipate.

I go back in time to those summer days, lying next to her, watching her, placing my hand over hers—pretending to admire her ring when all I really wanted was to touch her soft, delicate skin. In our family, we hardly touched; affection lived in acts of service, not in hugs or hand-holding. But in that quiet moment, the simple closeness meant everything. I soak in every second, knowing that time with her is fleeting and precious. I know there will come a day when I won't be here with her like this—surrounded by her light, powdery scent, the cool touch of her *batik duster*, her house dress.

Like bubbles of memories, they appear and disappear, float and pop. They come from every corner of my mind—unexpected and surprising at times: when I'm waiting in line, when I go for a walk, when I'm in school, when I'm about to fall asleep on my own bed. When I feel lonely for her.

These memories remind me that here, I was safe and loved. That no matter what was happening outside, when I stepped into *Emak's* room, nothing could touch me. Everything was good here. I can still hear her strong voice—yelling, laughing at the television, and telling her stories. Her stories, punctuated every so often with a *ngerti nggak*? Do you understand? She would tell stories about us, about her youth, about my grandpa—my *engkong*—and how they met. My favorite story is the one where I begged her to take me to Singapore the night before she left with my two siblings, when I was three years old.

"*Melok mak,*" I pleaded in Javanese. I want to come.

"Lu sek cilik! Nanti nangis, carik mami." She replied. You're still too little! You're going to cry for your mom.

"*Ngak, mak, ngak nangis,*" No, grandma. I won't cry, as I pleaded through my tears.

She smiled, resigned—never one to say no to any of her grandkids—and bought a ticket for me to join my siblings on our trip to Singapore, our new home. For the record, I never cried for my mom.

I go back to the foot massages she would give us grandkids on her bed as we pretended to watch overdramatic Indonesian soap operas. She took turns kneading our little feet, even though we should have been the ones massaging her old, tired feet. But she did it every night—fifteen minutes for each of us. Still, it was her stories we were more interested in paying attention to.

I return to *Emak's* room time and time again. It was my childhood. The home that I never lived in, but always come back to. What is home but where you feel loved, safe, and protected? In our home in Singapore, we were often alone. No mother or father around. Just their shadows.

Again and again I open the dark wooden door of *Emak's* room and hear the familiar sound of the screen door's hinge. The sound it makes as I push through to feel the first blast of air-conditioning in this impossibly hot and humid Indonesian climate.

I feel the carpet under my feet, rough, thin. It's gray-green color inspires neither warmth nor beauty, yet everything in this room brings me comfort. This room is sacred and everything in it, dust balls and mold, has a place here.

A small statue of Christ with open arms welcomes me as he stands on a feux-European white end table with ornate gold trimmings; a remnant furniture piece from our old home on *Jalan Karimunjawa*. Bits and pieces out of place, with a different history, memory, as if taken out of context and dramatically inserted into a scene that they didn't belong to.

"There's a layer of dust on top of Jesus' head," I once said.

Emak's eyes grow big as she tries to see the truth in my words. She has been a devout Christian ever since I've known her, praying for hours several times a day, reading the Bible, taking notes, and going to *gereja,* church.

My mom quickly approaches Jesus and wipes off his dusty head with tissue.

"No, no, see, it's all better," she assures *Emak*. Crisis averted.

A broken white exercise bike that hasn't been used in over twenty years becomes a permanent furniture piece in the room, a watch guard standing in front of the full-length mirror that hides an industrial-size safe.

I return to her room again and again when I need to remember that she was there for me—that she still lives in me, even when she's no longer here with us. I come home to her in this very room, to remember what it felt like to be loved, and to remind myself how I can continue living in her love.

I remind myself of the details.

The rack where she hung her worn clothes because wearing it all day didn't mean it was dirty yet, even though its odor told us otherwise. The neat stack of thick, fancy shopping bags, piled on top of a filing cabinet in the corner. Never used, but it was *eman,* a pity, to throw it away. Surely, it will be used one day. Her large closet was filled with custom-made clothes in every color and fabric, tailored to fit her perfectly as she went to work at the hospital each day. All of them made by the same seamstress, Sylvie, to suit her larger frame. Her white vanity set with the large oval mirror and a red-cushioned chair that was always too heavy to move. Yellow bottles of Vaseline, containers of *Oil of Ulay, La Tulipe* skincare, neat rows of pointy-shaped lipsticks, compact powders, half-finished bottles of perfume, framed photos of her grandkids, bottles of L'Oreal hairspray, a tissue box covered in an ornate fake gold gilded container. A golden clock of a boy holding the time, which has long stopped. The boombox with the same stack of dusty CDs—a collection of Michael Bolton and Kenny G. The stack of church programs and prayer booklets, next to the Bible that used to be opened twice a day, but has remained closed in recent years—her eyes strained to read and her mind lost in repeated thoughts. Walls covered with our family photos of summer days. When *Emak* gave us free rein to express ourselves through art classes, hours of playing video games, shopping for stationary, and choosing ribbons in *Pasar*

Atum, the local market, to make hair accessories to sell to our friends back in Singapore.

This is the room where she strutted like a proud peacock. This is where she enveloped us with her love. This room covered in details. This room, a museum of all things past and present, punctuations from the various stages of our lives.

The room where she died.

She was never the same after her stroke. She repeated her questions like a broken record. She forgot everything. Words slipped away. Her life no longer felt like her own. She was a passenger, trapped on a bus that never stopped—looking out the window, watching life pass her by. And then, during COVID-19, it was time to make a stop. To make the choice to get off the bus. To pull the cord, step off, and finally rest. To begin the next journey.

I want to be there. I am there. In my head. In her final moments. I imagine lying next to her in the very same spot. She lies next to me on the left side of the bed. I take my place. Lying next to her, watching her, just like my summer days.

"Thank you, *Emak*," I imagine telling her. "Thank you for everything you've done for me, everything you've taught me. Thank you for embracing me with your love. I never knew love like yours. I will carry it with me wherever I go."

Her eyes close, her chest rises and falls, struggling to catch her breath, her mind ready to meet my *engkong*, her husband, once again. A long-awaited reunion over twenty-five years after his death.

"*Emak pergi sek. Nanti aku melok.*" You go first, *Emak*. I'll follow you later.

I watch her as she takes her last breath that early morning. I hold *Emak's* hand, one last time, savoring the moment.

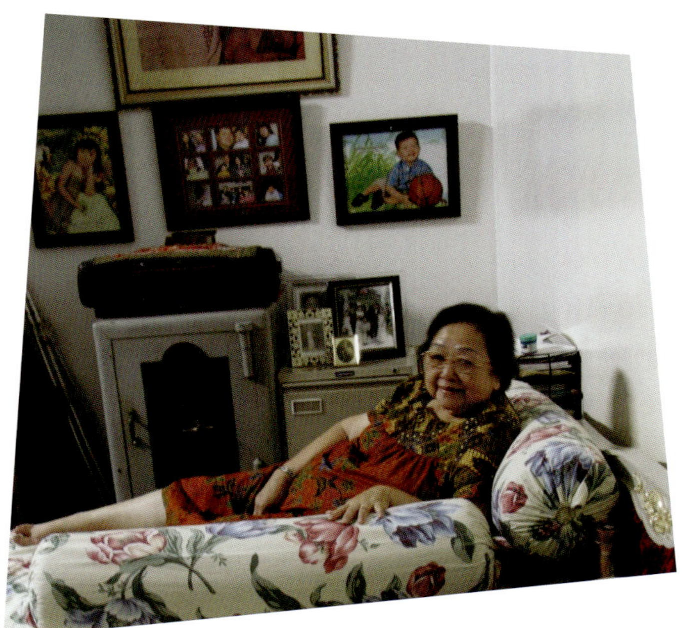

My *Emak* in her room, Surabaya, Indonesia.
Photo by Margaret Kerrison

Making Meaning

"Art holds out the promise of inner wholeness."

Alain de Botton and John Armstrong,
Art as Therapy

We often speak of cities as structures—systems of transit, buildings of concrete and steel, blueprints made real. Environmental settings where our lives occur. But when we walk through a city we love, we are not charting a path through infrastructure. We are moving through memory.

Urban spaces are not just built; they are felt. They carry the imprints of laughter, longing, love, and loss. And at the heart of these feelings is placemaking—the thoughtful creation and curation of spaces that invite people to not just use them, but to belong to them and become a part of their everyday lives.

Placemaking is not merely the arrangement of benches and pathways. It is the art of emotional engineering. It asks: how can we turn space into place? How do we transform the forgotten into the beloved? How can we create places that we love and protect?

Public art, sculpture, and utility play a vital role in transforming shared spaces. When a piece of art enters a public setting, it begins as an offering—and soon becomes a dialogue. Its significance is shaped by the public: they determine whether it becomes meaningful or fades into obscurity. Is it accessible, authentic, and connected to the community's identity? Does it grow and evolve alongside the people it represents?

When I was an undergrad at Tufts University, there was a cannon sculpture in our quad that was routinely "vandalized." Layers of paint from previous students revealed the evolving history of the piece—a replica of a twenty-four-pound cannon from the *USS Constitution*. Students were free to paint over it, leave their mark, and make it their own. It was an open invitation for creativity and expression. It served as a canvas for political messages. It belonged to the students—to use as they wished.

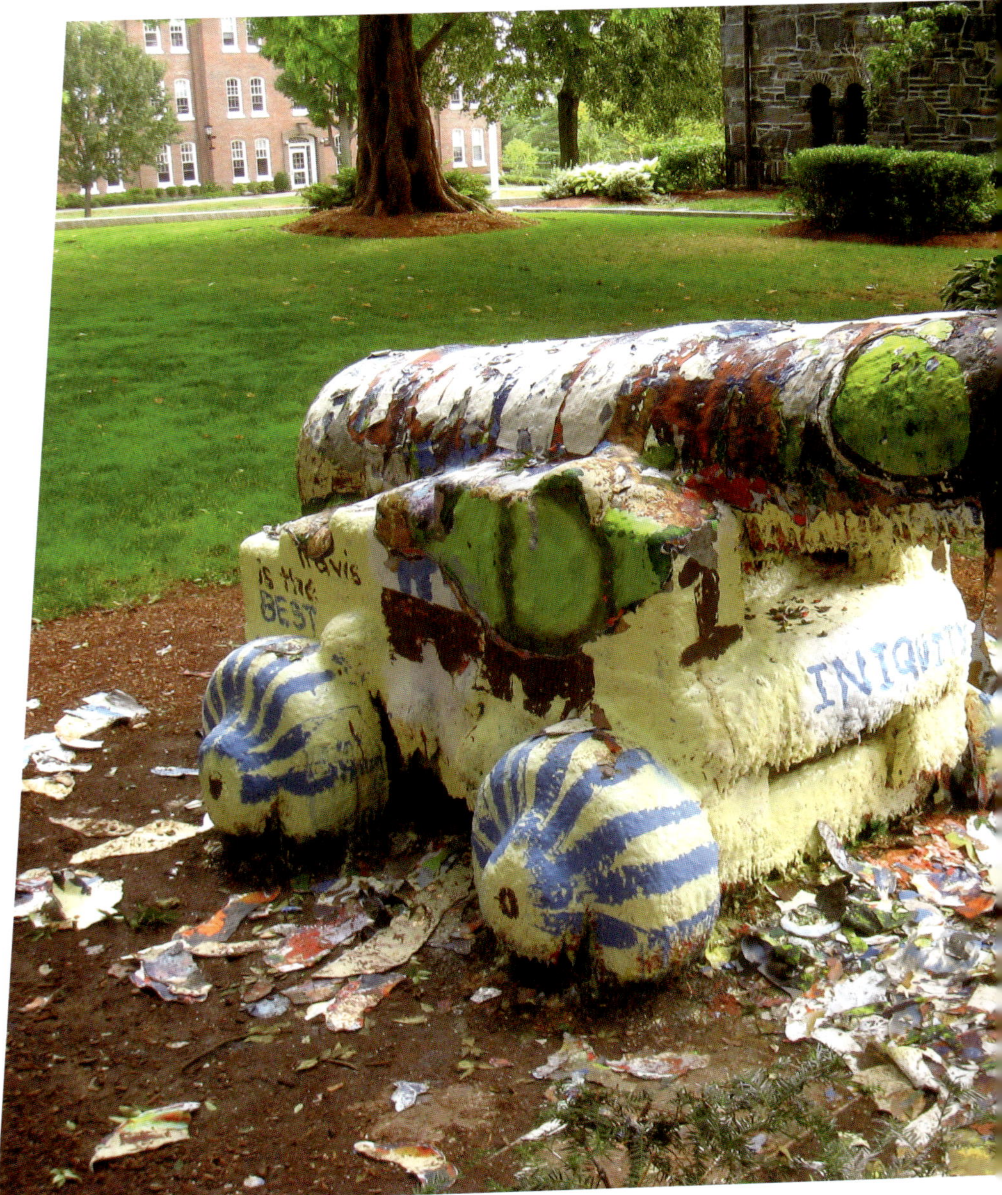
is the
BEST

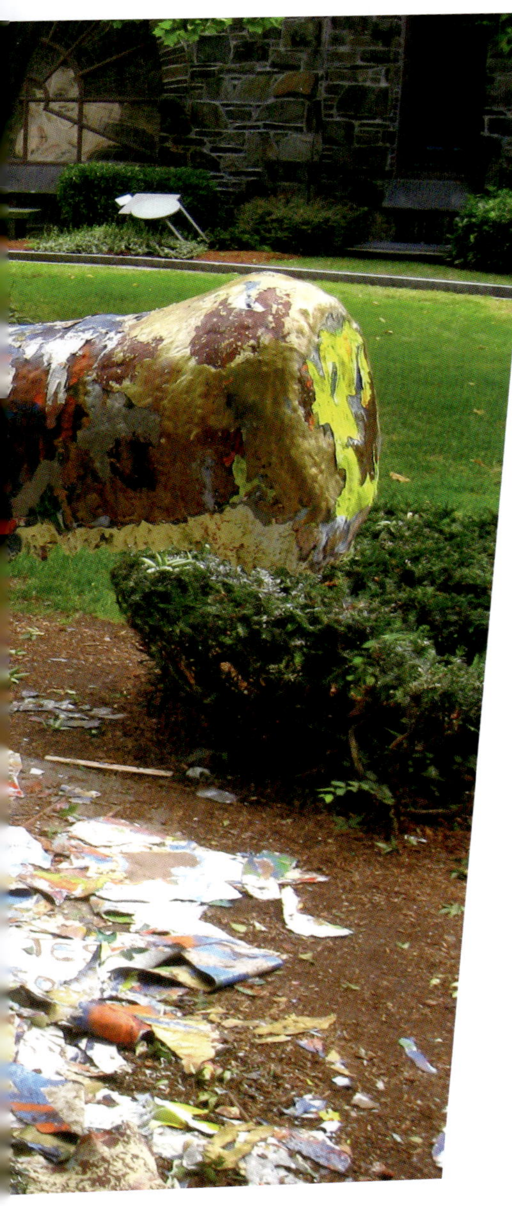

The Cannon at Tufts University in Medford, Massachusetts, photographed on August 15, 2010. Photo by Daderot (public domain)

Over time, sculptures like these become more than just "the sculpture in the park." They become *ours*—the one we grew up with, the one we passed every morning on the way to class, the one glowing with winter lights, the one we posed with for selfies when family and friends came to visit.

I remember how, during the dark, harsh New England winters, when I felt lonely and depressed, I would look for that cannon. It became a quiet witness—a reminder that I was still here, that there was something familiar to hold on to. In a way, it felt like it was looking out for me, too.

Once the public has access to something meaningful—whether a sculpture, a mural, a performance space, or a quiet shaded bench—they begin to see themselves in it. They claim it not through possession, but through presence. It becomes a keeper of their memories and a fixture in their rituals.

Like a particular bench under a shaded oak tree at the Huntington Library in San Marino, CA—one that we regard as our "anniversary bench." This is where my husband and I took photos for our five-year anniversary with our photographer friend. It's where we often sat, and still sit, to enjoy the view. Years later, it became the place where we brought our son to sit and play in the grass.

This bench is more than just a place to rest—it's a holder, a time machine, a keeper of our memories. A reminder of where we came from, where we are, and where we're going. A silent witness to our fleeting, precious lives.

We see this phenomenon play out vividly in places like Disneyland. As storytellers and designers of immersive worlds, we've learned that even the smallest design choices can become sacred. The removal of a familiar bench. A subtle change in a beloved attraction's story. The addition of an audio-animatronic to a classic ride. A weathered sign that's remained untouched for decades. To an outsider, these details may seem insignificant—but to a guest who returns regularly, they are emotional anchors. Changing them isn't just a matter of redesign or upkeep; it's a disruption of a personal narrative. And that disruption is felt deeply.

Cities are not so different. When a mural is painted over, when a beloved bowling alley is replaced by modern condos, or when the shade tree is removed from a park corner, the community doesn't just lose utility—it loses a piece of its collective soul.

That's why placemaking must be rooted in memory—not in nostalgia for its own sake, but in a shared reverence for meaning. When we design urban spaces with intention and invite the community to co-author their environments, we create places that are not just beautiful, but beloved. These places become protectable. Defendable. Not because they are costly or grand, but because they belong to the people.

There is a subtle yet powerful shift that happens when people identify with the places they inhabit. They begin to care. To participate. To steward. That's when true sustainability happens—not just environmentally, but culturally. Cities must be planned for longevity, yes—but they must also be planned for love.

Public art and the spaces they inhabit are more than decoration—they are catalysts for connection. They guide us not only through physical space but also through emotional landscapes. They help us understand where we are—and more importantly, who we are in that place, in that moment.

As designers, artists, and stewards of the built environment, our role is to listen deeply—to create with empathy. To imagine not only what a space can hold, but what it can mean. Our task is to shape places that invite belonging—places with the potential to be loved and honored by collective caretakers. Because the most successful public spaces aren't grand spectacles—they're felt. They're the ones people return to, care for, and pass down through generations.

When a place becomes personal, it becomes sacred. And sacred spaces, once given, must be honored. That is the power of placemaking—and the responsibility of those who shape public space.

Designing For CRISIS

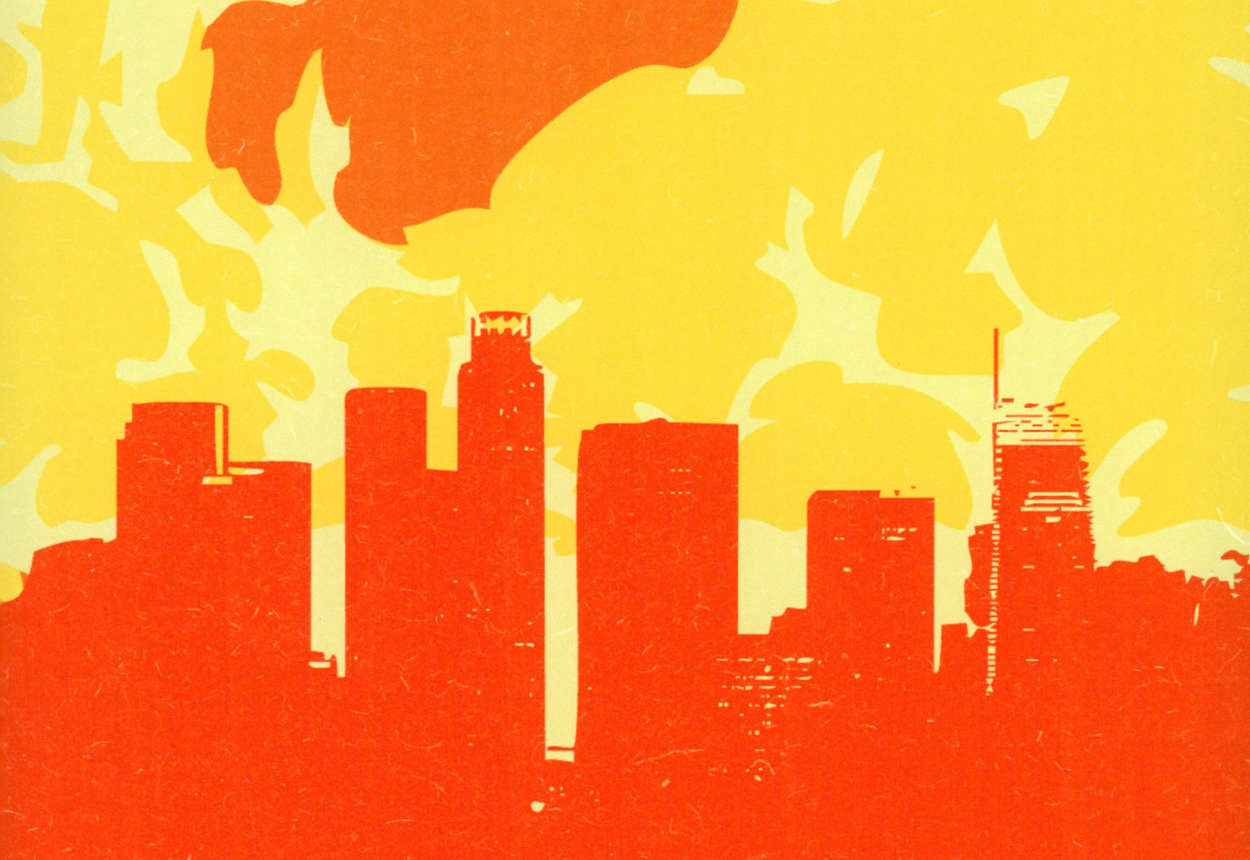

This past winter session, I had the opportunity to teach an *Immersive Worldbuilding* seminar at the California Institute of the Arts. The course was initially planned as an in-person experience, focused on building fictional worlds as a tool for creative exploration and design thinking. But just as we were about to begin, another wildfire broke out in Santa Clarita—forcing us to shift the course to a remote format. The irony was hard to ignore: we were preparing to teach about speculative futures when our own reality was being reshaped by a climate disaster.

Rather than seeing this disruption as a setback, I decided to reframe it as a challenge for the students. In light of the wildfires and growing climate emergencies in California, I asked the class to consider a vital question: What can designers do in the face of climate change? We may not be first responders, but that doesn't mean we're powerless. As designers, we have the ability to shape narratives, environments, and emotional experiences that can inspire change. As students, they had the perfect platform to imagine how their creativity could contribute to a better, more resilient world.

I offered the class two project options. Option 1 was open-ended: design any immersive experience of their choice. But in response to the fires and ongoing climate disruptions, I introduced Option 2: Design an Immersive Climate Change Experience. To my surprise—and encouragement—Option 2 became the most popular choice. Many students were eager to grapple with the issues unfolding around them and use their skills to engage with real-world challenges.

For those who chose Option 2, the assignment was to create a fictional or nonfictional immersive attraction that explores the impact of climate change on urban cities like Los Angeles. The setting could be in the present, near future, or distant future. Their job was not just to speculate but to engage—emotionally, intellectually, and socially—with the real-world implications of climate change.

Students explored questions like: What does a climate-ravaged Los Angeles look like? Is it underwater from sea level rise, or a deserted metropolis choked by sandstorms? Have some neighborhoods been abandoned or overtaken by nature?

Each project required a "core experience"—anything from a guided museum exhibit of vanished neighborhoods recreated through holograms, to a VR simulation where guests navigate a future megacity as climate refugees, to a participatory theater performance set during an extreme heatwave.

I was deeply inspired by the students' creativity and how thoughtfully they wove their personal experiences into their work. One group created a haunting journey through a future world devastated by climate inaction, urging participants to confront the consequences of complacency. Another group developed a vibrant, child-focused educational model that celebrated the natural world—designed to help young audiences fall in love with nature in order to protect it. Yet another team brought a whimsical approach to the challenge, crafting an imaginative adventure through fantastical worlds, each hosted by unique characters that made the climate message both fun and memorable.

These projects were more than creative exercises—they were acts of resilience, empathy, and vision. They reminded me that design is never just about aesthetics or functionality; it's about connection. In times of crisis, when the future feels uncertain, designers have a unique role to play: to help communities reimagine what's possible, to tell stories that move people, and to inspire action. Even in the midst of wildfires and over the limitations of Zoom, these students rose to the occasion. They imagined better futures—and, in doing so, began to build them.

As designers, we may not be first responders, but we are still essential. In the wake of the fires, I saw friends step up—volunteering architectural support, drafting rebuilding plans, and helping neighbors navigate the complexities of insurance and construction. It was a powerful reminder: we are problem solvers. We turn uncertainty into opportunity, ideas into form, and visions into lived experience. When the world is in flux, it needs more creative minds willing to chart a new course. Where others see dead ends, we see new paths forward—and the courage to build them.

THE NEUTRA VDL HOUSE:

A Story Of Resilience And Renewal

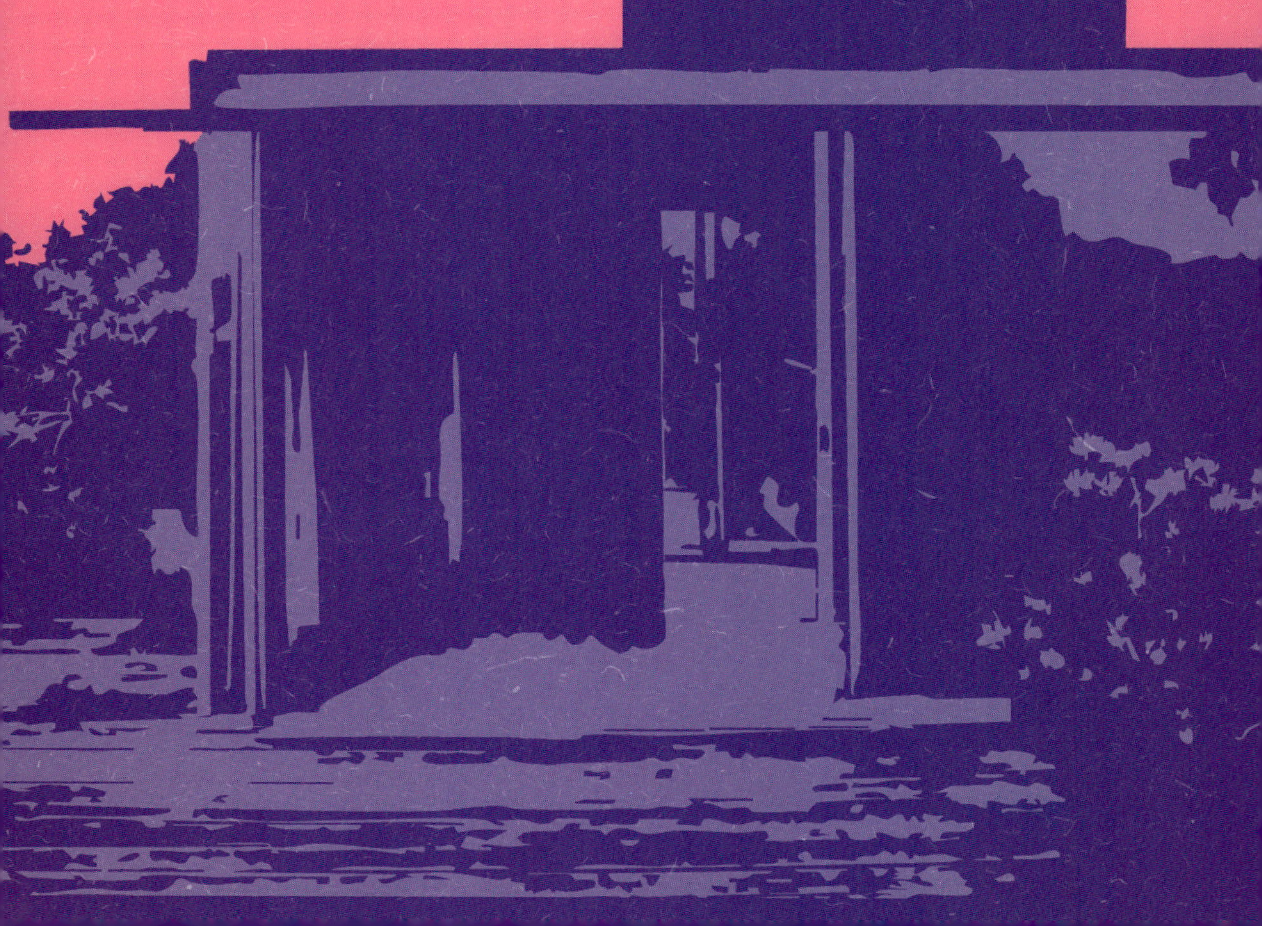

Two years ago, during my Paul Helmle Fellowship, I spent a couple of weekends visiting the Neutra VDL Studio and Residences in Silver Lake while leading workshops for Cal Poly Pomona architecture students on the art of immersive storytelling. I was struck by its history—a house once consumed by fire, now rebuilt. Yes, the Neutra House fell victim to what was perhaps an electrical fire, but the story of fires is an inescapable part of life in Los Angeles, which is bone-dry and has a Mediterranean climate—so much so that we often forget how many before us have had to start anew from the ashes.

I've lived in LA for over twenty years, but the recent wildfires of January 2024 were truly unprecedented. Thousands were displaced in Altadena and the Pacific Palisades as the fires swept through quickly and furiously in the early morning. Most are now living in temporary housing, trying to rebuild their lives and asking big questions that will shape their next chapter.

Los Angeles is a city constantly in flux, shaped by cycles of destruction and renewal. Its landscape is defined by reinvention, whether through natural disasters, urban expansion, or cultural evolution. Few places embody this spirit of resilience more powerfully than the Neutra VDL House—an architectural landmark that serves as both a living artifact of modernist history and a testament to enduring creative resolve.

Richard Neutra originally designed the house in 1932 in the International Style as both his home and architectural office, naming it after benefactor Dr. C. H. Van Der Leeuw.

Beyond serving as his family's residence, it was also a model for innovative small-lot construction, proving that modern design could bring nature indoors while maintaining privacy even in dense urban settings. The house functioned as a living laboratory where Neutra explored ideas about space, light, and human-centered design.

It's no wonder that every time I visited the Neutra VDL House, I felt uplifted—surrounded by nature, with natural sunlight streaming through the large windows, creating a sanctuary in a city that never seems to quiet down. Here, I felt at peace and safe. It's not my home, and yet it offers a sense of welcome and security that most houses lack.

In 1963, a devastating fire reduced most of the original structure to ashes. When Neutra returned a week later from his trip to assess the damage, he despaired: "It is all over, there will be no way to reconstruct this ruin."

At seventy-one years old, he faced an immense loss—not just of his home but of the archive stored in the basement: three decades of drawings, documents, and mementos chronicling his life and career. Yet, despite this profound setback, he chose to rebuild. With his son and architectural partner, Dion Neutra, he embarked on the design of a new house that would carry forward the spirit of the original while embracing fresh innovations.

Between 1964 and 1968, the Neutras reimagined a home not just with walls and windows, but with intention—a living, breathing space that invited light, reflection, and thought. The VDL Research House II rose gently from the remains of its predecessor, a glass-and-wood sanctuary anchored by its original concrete foundation. Here, architecture became experience. The transparency of the glass, the seamless integration of built-in furnishings, and the carefully placed mirrors worked in harmony to stretch the limits of space and perception.

But this second iteration wasn't merely a reconstruction—it was an evolution. Cantilevered balconies reached outward like open arms. Rooftop reflecting pools blurred the line between sky and structure. Inside and outside spoke to each other in natural dialogue. If the first VDL House hinted at the possibilities of modernist living on a small urban lot, this new version made a bolder, more confident statement—one that looked toward the future without forgetting its roots.

More than an architectural feat, the home became a conversation between father and son. Richard and Dion Neutra's collaboration fused two visions into one living story—an expression of legacy, growth, and the enduring belief that great design can nourish the human spirit.

The story of the Neutra VDL House is emblematic of Los Angeles's broader struggle with natural disasters, particularly wildfires, which have become an enduring and intensifying threat. The city's topography, climate, and urban sprawl make it especially vulnerable to fires that indiscriminately consume homes, businesses, and landmarks.

Yet time and again, its residents rebuild—with a defiance and determination that propel them forward despite their losses. The Neutra family's decision to reconstruct their home rather than abandon it reflects a deeply ingrained ethos of resilience that runs through Los Angeles's history. This is a city that doesn't merely endure destruction—it reimagines itself in the wake of adversity.

Beyond its symbolic significance, the Neutra VDL House continues to serve a vital role in contemporary discourse on architecture and urban sustainability. In 1990, Richard Neutra's wife, Dione, bequeathed the VDL Research House II to Cal Poly Pomona's College of Environmental Design. Today, the house remains not just a historical landmark but an active space for research, education, and public engagement. It hosts regular tours, design workshops, and artist residencies, ensuring that Neutra's legacy continues to inspire new generations. Its continued existence underscores the importance of preservation—not just of physical structures but of the ideals they represent. The house remains a living testament to the notion that architecture is not static; it is an evolving dialogue between past and future, destruction and renewal.

The Neutra VDL House stands as a reminder that loss is not always final; it can be an opportunity for reinvention, a reaffirmation of vision and purpose. Just as Los Angeles continually reconstructs itself in response to challenges, so too does this iconic structure, proving that resilience is not just an architectural principle but a way of life.

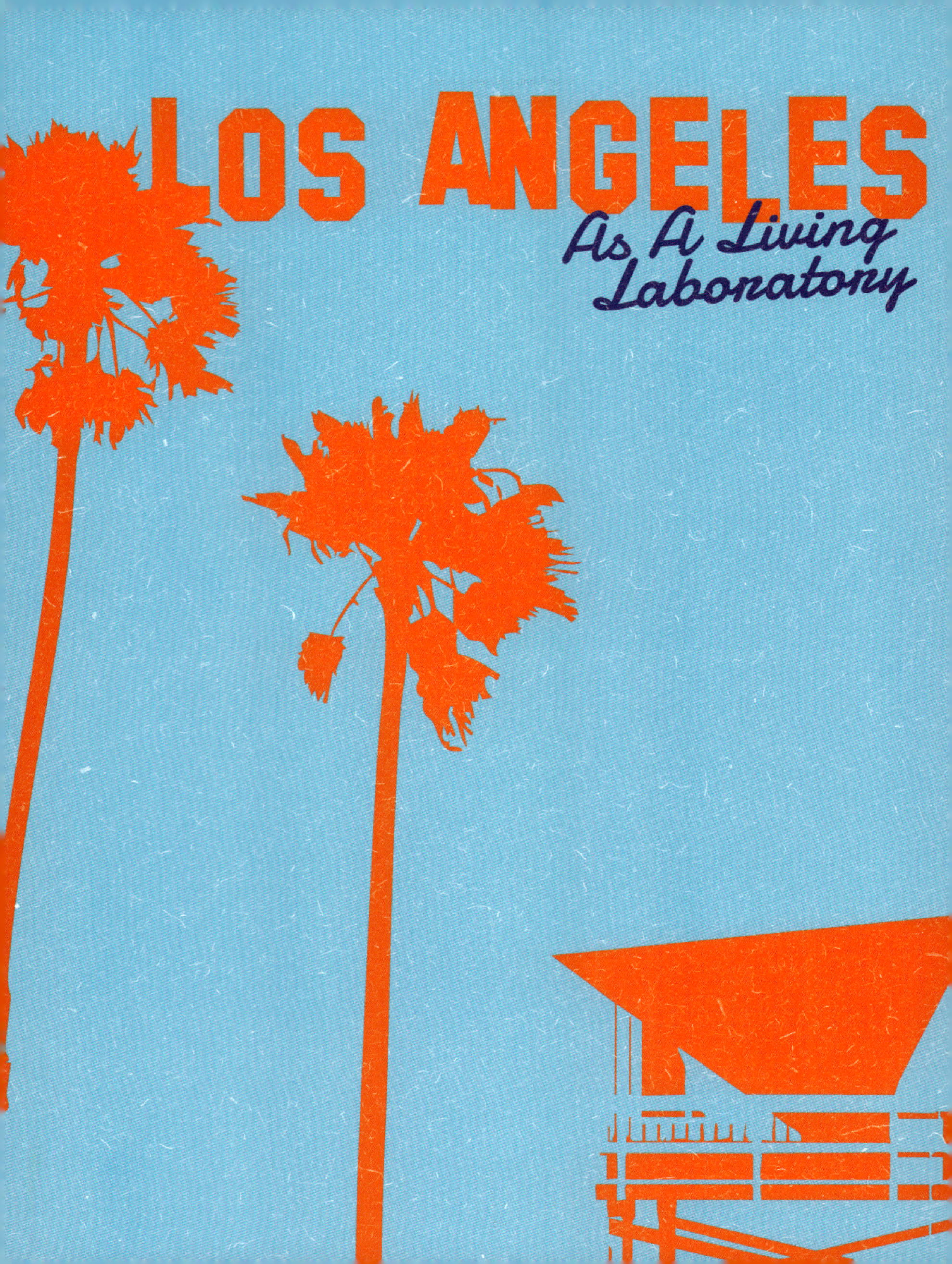

LOS ANGELES

As A Living Laboratory

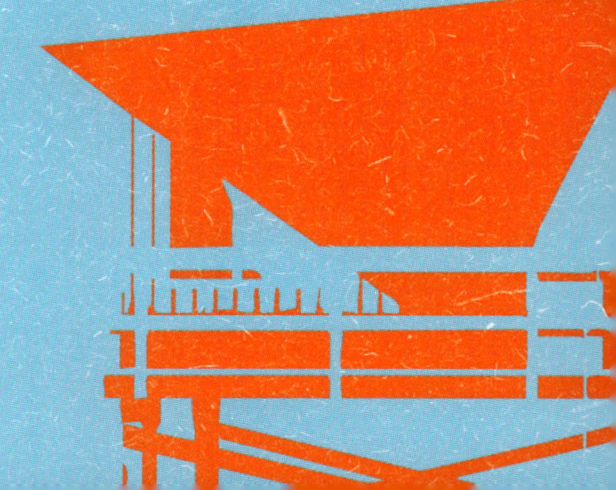

Everyone around me seemed to know exactly who they were, what they were doing, and where they were going—or at least, that's how it looked from the outside. That was my impression when I was twenty-six years old, newly married, and standing at the edge of a new chapter in a new city. My husband and I had just moved across the country to Los Angeles, a city teeming with movement, ambition, and invention. To me, it was more than a city—it was a wide-open laboratory for life, a place where the rules could be rewritten, where identities were fluid, and where dreams didn't just live—they were performed with fervor. It was a place for rebels, rascals, and rule-breakers. It was the perfect place for me.

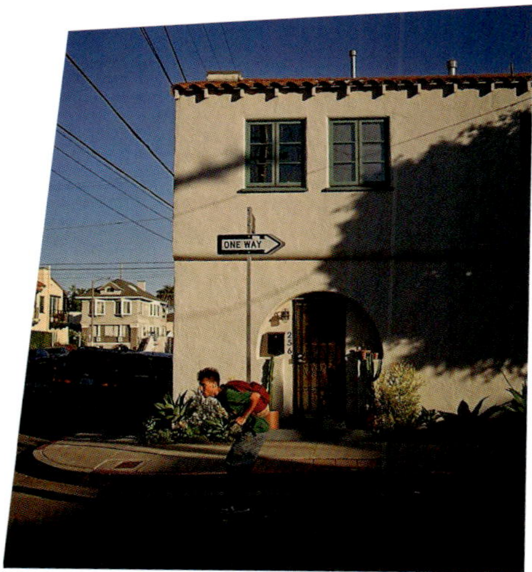

LA street scene.
Photo by Foster Kerrison

This was where I had decided to throw my cards in the air, let them scatter, and see where they landed. I didn't have a set plan, but that was the plan. I wanted to experiment—try on new identities, step into unfamiliar roles, chase unexpected paths. I didn't have a road map when I came to LA, just two questions: What if? Why not?

The journey was supposed to begin before we arrived. My husband and I had planned a spontaneous, unstructured cross-country road trip

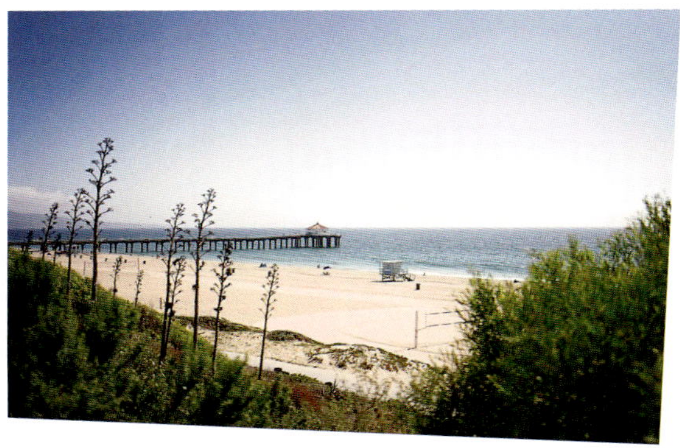

Southern California's coastline.
Photos by Foster Kerrison

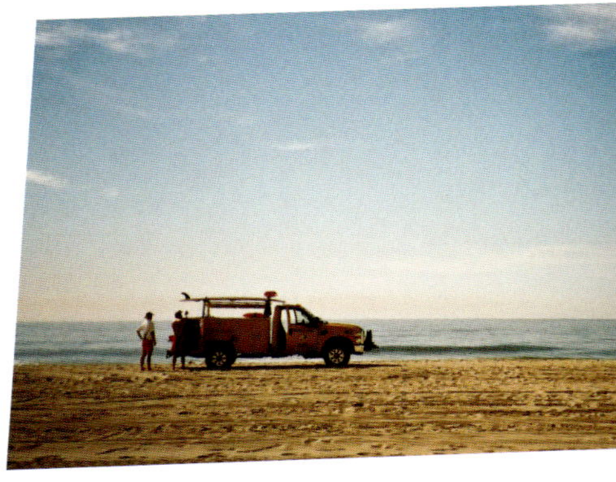

from Boston to Los Angeles. We didn't book any hotel rooms. We didn't have planned routes. We imagined a week of wandering—driving through small towns, staying in roadside motels with flickering neon signs, eating at diners that felt like movie sets. We had no real itinerary, just curiosity as our compass and the thrill of seeing where the road would literally and figuratively take us. That drive was meant to be a slow transition into our new life—an adventure in itself.

But the road trip never happened. On the very first day, as we made our way to our first stop—my in-laws' house—we were rear-ended while turning a corner. In an instant, our plans scattered. The car was damaged, the trip called off. That was our first lesson in the journey ahead: sometimes—often—plans don't unfold the way you imagine. So,

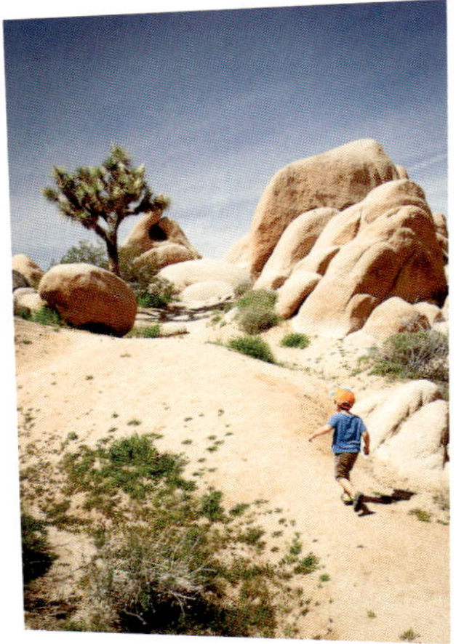

Joshua Tree National Park.
Photos by Foster Kerrison

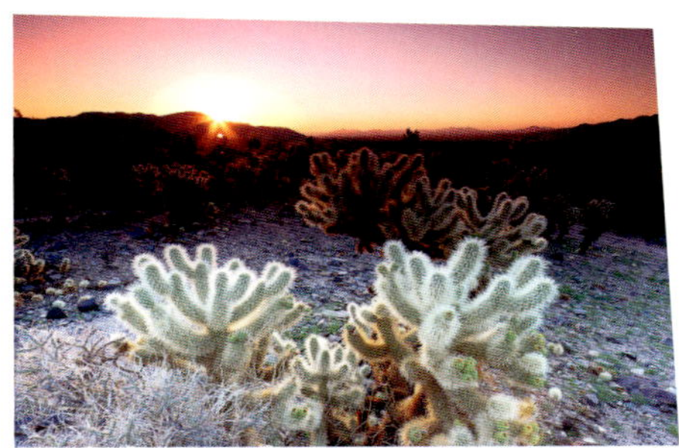

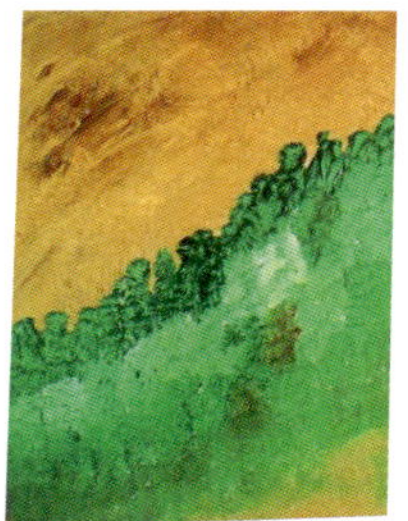

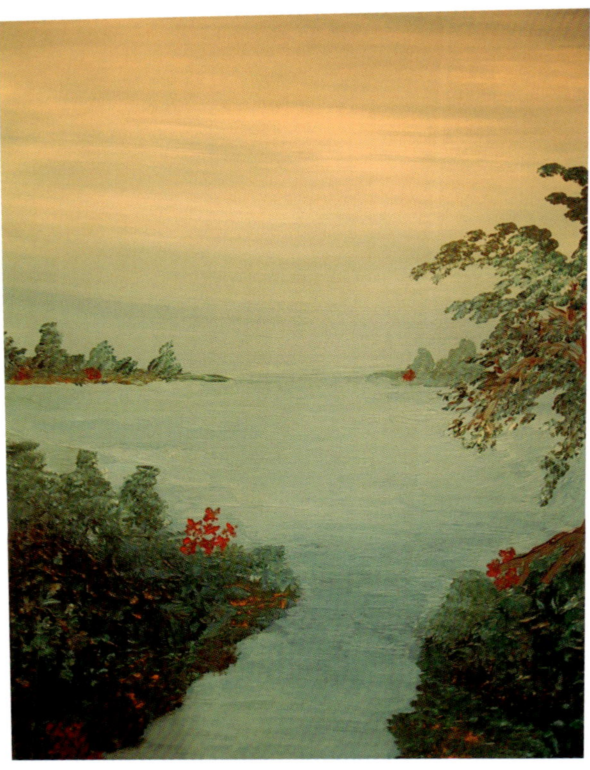

My early acrylic paintings after arriving in LA.
Photos by Margaret Kerrison

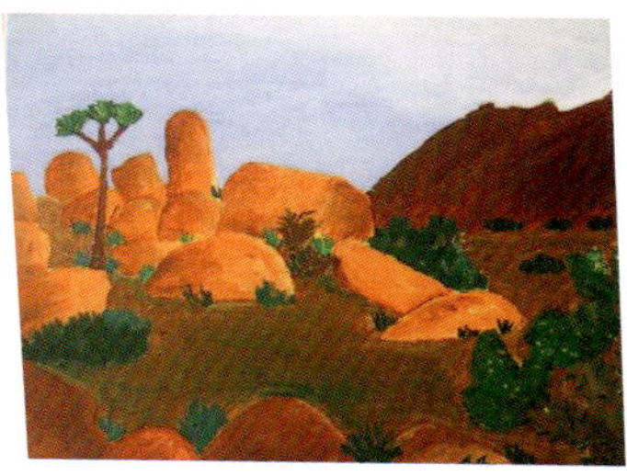

instead of driving across the country, we booked a flight. We arrived in Los Angeles earlier than expected, not with a sense of adventure, but with the quiet realization that the unknown had already begun.

Once we arrived in Los Angeles, we landed in a modest, slightly worn one-bedroom apartment in the Fairfax District, just south of Wilshire Boulevard. Our belongings were sparse—since we were waiting for most of our possessions to arrive in a moving container one week later, presumably after we finished our road trip. We slept on a newly purchased mattress on the floor, the kind of beginning that feels temporary, yet deeply memorable.

The apartment had a small balcony that overlooked a courtyard filled with a huge tree that we soon realized housed an army of ants. Nevertheless, that balcony became my first studio. I unpacked my acrylic paints and started to make sense of my new life in color. I painted the landscapes we had just seen—Joshua Tree's unusual spires, Malibu's golden sunsets and hiking trails, the sleepy towns along the Central Coast. The canvas helped me process what I didn't yet have words for: liberation, transition, becoming, evolution.

But painting wasn't the only form of expression I experimented with. I wrote screenplays. Or tried to. Each morning, I opened my laptop and imagined characters who, like me, were trying to find their footing in an unfamiliar world. I wasn't working yet—my US citizenship paperwork was still being processed—so my days were filled with unpaid internships that felt like a makeshift play. I threw myself into every role like it was a starring performance.

At a literary agency in Beverly Hills, I answered phones (poorly, I might add) and welcomed visitors with a nervous smile. I read stacks of scripts, learning how stories were structured and what made them sellable—or not. I wrote coverage—summaries and critiques—dreaming of the day someone might be reading my work with the same hopeful attention. I wasn't getting paid, but I was getting a front-row view into a world I longed to be part of.

At the same time, I took an internship at an interior design firm in Century City. I found myself flipping through fabric swatches, touching silks and velvets with curiosity. I walked the halls of the Pacific Design

Center like I belonged there, imagining spaces not yet real. It was a world of textures and palettes and possibilities. I didn't know if I was truly cut out for it—but I leaned in anyway. An intuitive in Boston had once told me I'd be "designing environments," a phrase that sounded strange and abstract at the time. "You'll be working with color and space," she said. I didn't know what it meant then, but I remembered her words as I experimented with everything from *feng shui* to collage cork boards filled with cutout design and architecture magazine images of other peoples' homes.

That year was a personal renaissance—an invitation to explore, to fail, to reimagine. Los Angeles wasn't just a city. It was a living lab, a sandbox, a canvas with infinite possibilities. Here, you could test an idea without needing to defend it. Or be judged. No one judges you here. They believe you even before you earn the role. Everyone here wants to believe. They want to believe you're going to be the next undiscovered screenwriter to make them rich. They want to believe they found the next Jon M. Chu or Selena Gomez. They want to believe that they had a pivotal part to play in the next blockbuster or bestseller. They are all dreamers and believers. You could be a writer on Monday, a designer by Wednesday, and something entirely new by the end of the week. Nothing was locked in. Nothing had to last. And there was something liberating about that.

Back in Boston, the first questions were usually, "Where are you from?" and "What college do you go to?" In LA, the questions were, "Where do you live?" and "What do you do?" I soon realized that beneath the surface, there always seemed to be two more unspoken questions lingering in people's minds: "Who do you know?" and "What can you do for me?" I came to understand that friendships were often predetermined by your zip code—no one wanted to drive to an area they didn't live in. It raised an important question: Is this friendship worth sitting through rush hour?

In those early days of living in LA, I didn't earn a paycheck, so there was no pressure to commit. I floated from one experience to the next—a few weeks here, a couple months there. I didn't know then how rare that kind of freedom would be. I wasn't a full-time student or employee anymore. I wasn't a mother yet. I wasn't anyone's responsibility. I was just me, in flux, searching. That time—so rich with uncertainty and possibility—would come to feel like a once-in-a-lifetime gift. A rare window where I was allowed to find myself on my own terms, without deadlines or expectations.

And LA was the perfect stage for that kind of becoming. This city didn't demand credentials, degrees, or pedigree. In fact, just like its Hollywood movies, it loved a good underdog story. LA welcomed the unusual, the unexpected, and the unique. It welcomed personal exploration. It whispered and beckoned: *Try it.* Play the part. See how it feels. You didn't need to audition to imagine yourself into a new life—you just needed the courage to show up.

Now, looking back, I see that year for what it truly was—not a detour, but a foundation for my fluid, ever-evolving sense of identity and constant search for belonging. A deeply formative season where I learned to trust my instincts, to follow what sparked joy and curiosity, even when I had no idea where it might lead. It was a year of becoming—messy, magical, and entirely mine.

Sunset over LAX.
Photo by Foster Kerrison

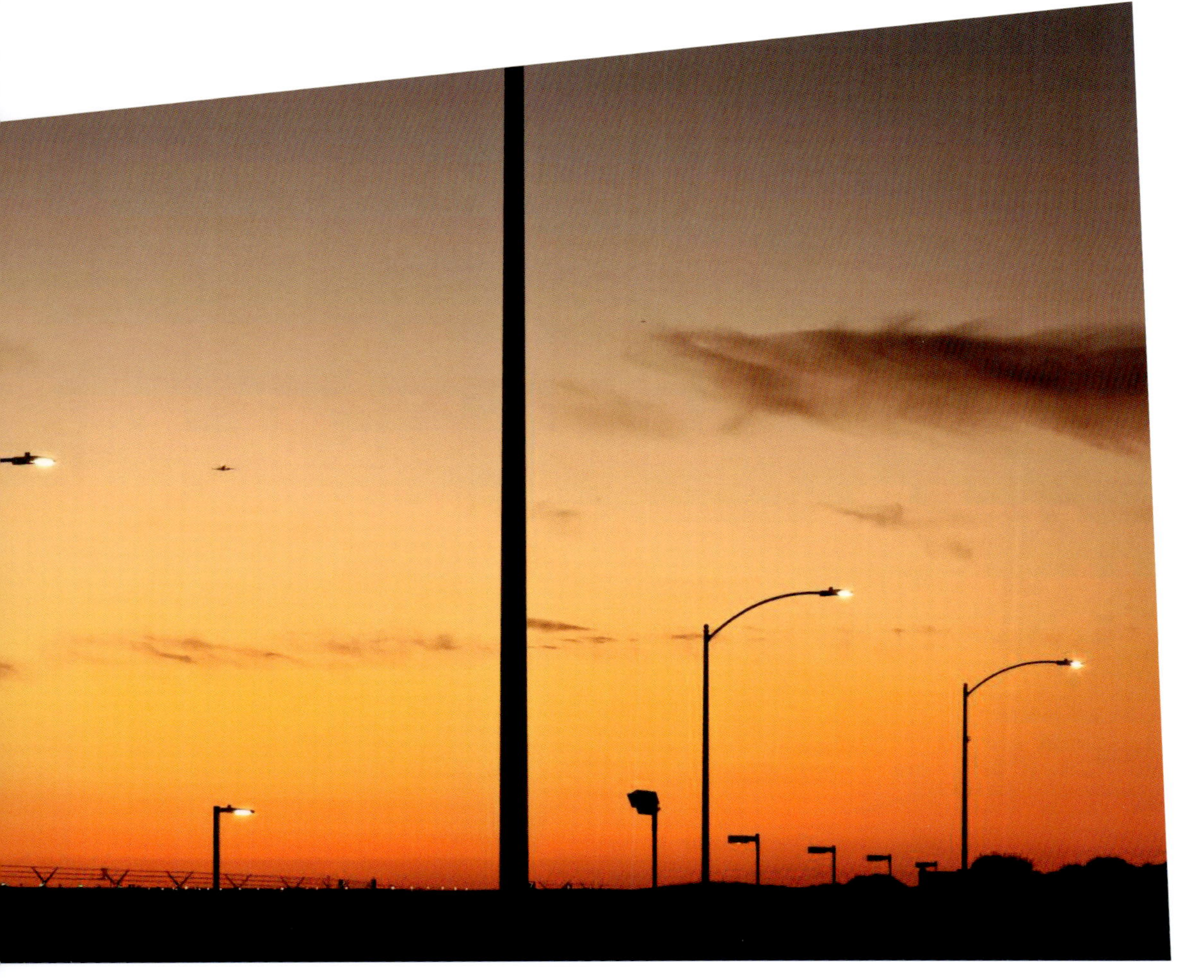

The Capital Of PLAY

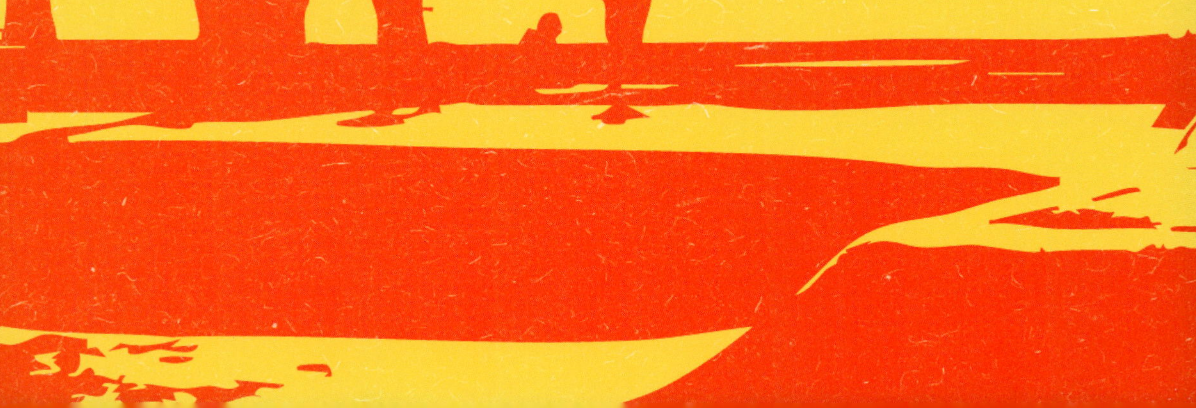

When I was a newly arrived immigrant to the United States, I developed blurry, broad definitions of American cities. Washington, DC was where people went to govern. New York was for fashion and finance. Boston was for studying. And Los Angeles? LA was for play—in every form. It was the land of endless play.

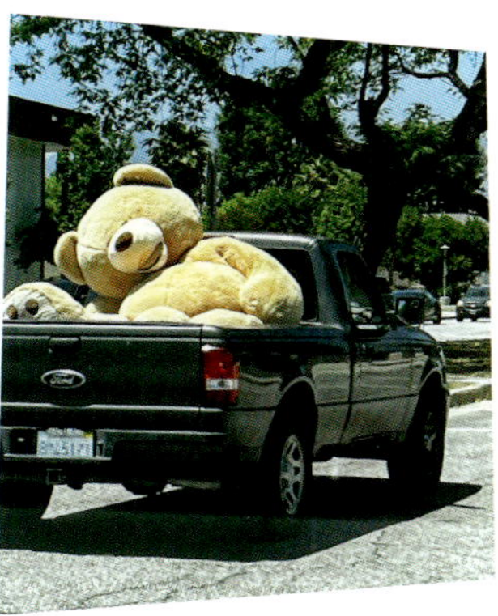

Giant teddy bear out for a ride.
Spotted in Pasadena, CA.
Photo by Bryce Kerrison

I first visited LA when I was eleven, accompanied by my family, our itinerary included the iconic theme parks: Disneyland, Universal Studios, Magic Mountain, and Knott's Berry Farm. If LA had a thesis, it was this—play wasn't just encouraged; it was institutionalized. For someone who valued play above all else, the city felt less like a destination and more like a premonition. In my handmade fourth-grade book (illustrated, I might add, with the confidence of a child unburdened by self-doubt), I wrote that one day, I would be a designer or architect living in Los Angeles, married, with two children. Most of that came true—except I only have one child.

21

Future Hopes

I hope to marry a man who cares and loves me and have two children, a girl and a boy. I hope to have a happy family and also hope we live in the United States or in Indonesia. We will have a maid that helps us with the housework.

I hope to live in Los Angeles or Surabaya Indonesia so I can visit my relatives. I would my children to go to school in United States.

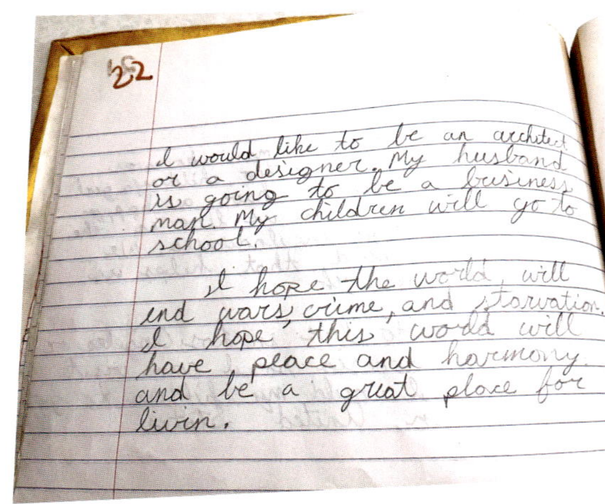

22

I would like to be an architect or a designer. My husband is going to be a business man. My children will go to school.

I hope the world will end wars, crime, and starvation. I hope this world will have peace and harmony and be a great place for livin.

The beginnings of a storyteller—my fourth grade book project. Photos by Margaret Kerrison

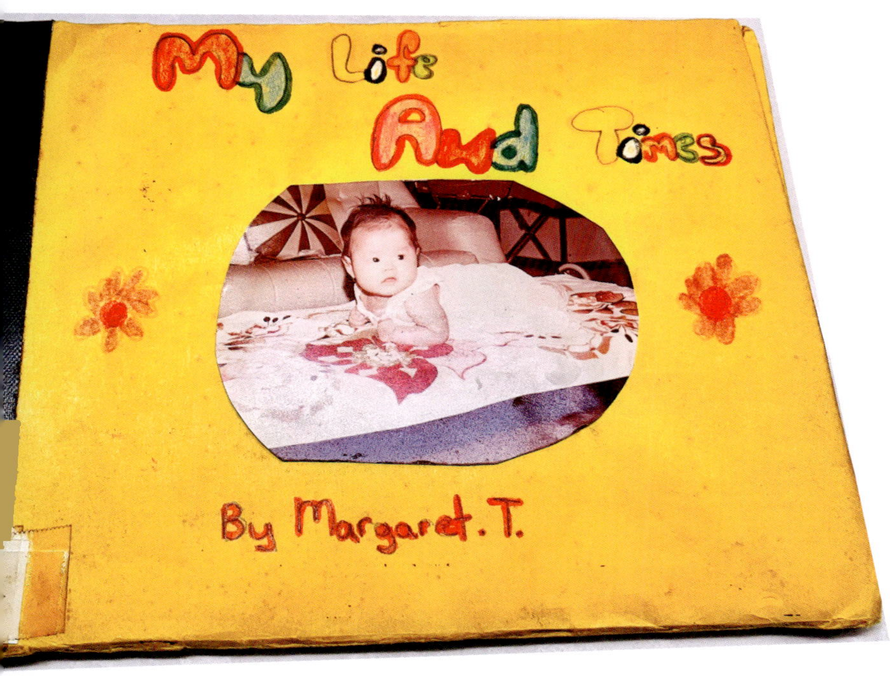

Now, as a middle-aged woman in LA, I can say I've fulfilled my childhood vision. I have played my part in the city where reinvention is both currency and requirement. This is a place where possibilities are as infinite as the freeways—provided, of course, that you can navigate the traffic. But that's the thing about LA. It rewards persistence. It is not, despite its palm-lined façades, for the faint of heart. The city belongs to those who can hear "no" a thousand times and still carry on with determination. To those who take rejection as a challenge to prove oneself. To those who, despite all evidence to the contrary, refuse to surrender the belief that the next audition, the next script, the next venture will be the one.

LA is often accused of immaturity and superficiality, but in truth, there is nothing unserious or shallow about its people. Don't believe for a second that when you hear Southern Californians speak in their lazy, Valley-inflected tongue, they are dumb. Quite the contrary—Angelenos are some of the cleverest people you'll ever meet. What makes them clever is that they don't play by the rules. They find shortcuts and ways to get over the fence. They are resilient enough to keep knocking on doors and to get up every time they're knocked down. They're boxers who don't know the physical limits of a ring and refuse to listen to the *ding ding ding* signaling the end of a round. The people drawn here believe in the power of a well-articulated dream and, even better, a successfully pitched one. They don't wait for fate to call—they cold-email, they network, they self-produce. The city's great secret is that "Fake it till you make it" isn't a punchline—it's a call to action. Or perhaps, more accurately: play the role you want until the role wants you back.

I played mine. I arrived in LA convinced I would be the next great American screenwriter. I even became American here, quite literally, naturalizing as a citizen in the LA Convention Center, where years ago, I had attended a screenwriting expo. I wandered museums, shops, beaches, K-town malls, visualizing my dream and making grand plans of finding my way into the entertainment industry. Then came the letter—my acceptance into USC's School of Cinematic Arts for an MFA in Screenwriting. I cried, believing (as one does at twenty-six) that this was the beginning of my inevitable rise.

For two years, I lived inside the USC bubble, a campus populated by the naively ambitious. We played at filmmaking with all the conviction of people certain they were destined for success. We wrote. We cast actors, filmed scenes, edited footage in dimly lit rooms, and screened our projects for each other with equal parts hope and critique. We were competitive. We believed in our own mythology.

My first job out of USC was as a researcher on the first season of "Wired Science," a KCET series in collaboration with PBS and *Wired* magazine. It was my first exposure to a universal truth: no one really knows what they're doing. The entire world, it turned out, was improvising. I made cold calls to scientists and engineers, convincing them to appear on our show. I pitched stories weekly, fabricating confidence as needed. I researched bridge engineering. I helped on set. I met Elon Musk before he was *Elon Musk*.

There were eight of us in a room the size of a large walk-in closet, talking into phones, typing furiously on our keyboards. We were all playing our parts. And somehow, improbably, we made it work.

My next job was with an experience design company that took a chance on me. I had zero experience designing museums and theme parks, yet they saw something in my writing samples (screenplays I wrote at USC), and my acrylic works. I even showed them my handmade greeting cards. They wanted to know how I thought, how I worked, whether I could write as well as express myself visually. They took me under their wing and I will forever be grateful.

In the years that followed, I began to see Los Angeles not just as a city, but as a stage—an ever-evolving playground where story and space intertwined. I learned how to shape physical environments that guided people with the same intuitive rhythm as a well-written screenplay. Like scenes in a film, every space had a story beat that moved visitors forward with purpose and momentum, echoing the kinetic energy of LA itself. Nothing was accidental; every visual, texture, sound, and scent had intention behind it, just like the layered worlds of film sets and theme parks this city is known for. Designing these immersive experiences became my way of playing with the city's storytelling DNA. This was where my passion began—when I realized that in LA, play isn't a distraction from meaning, it's how meaning is made.

Years later, I see that my childhood intuition about LA wasn't wrong—it is a city built on play, but play in its most determined, disciplined form. The kind that demands resilience, reinvention, and the willingness to embrace uncertainty. I may not have become the next great American screenwriter, but I became something better: a person who kept playing, kept writing, kept pushing forward. LA didn't hand me my dream on a silver platter; it asked if I was willing to earn it. And in answering that question, I became the version of myself that, at eleven years old, I somehow always knew I would be.

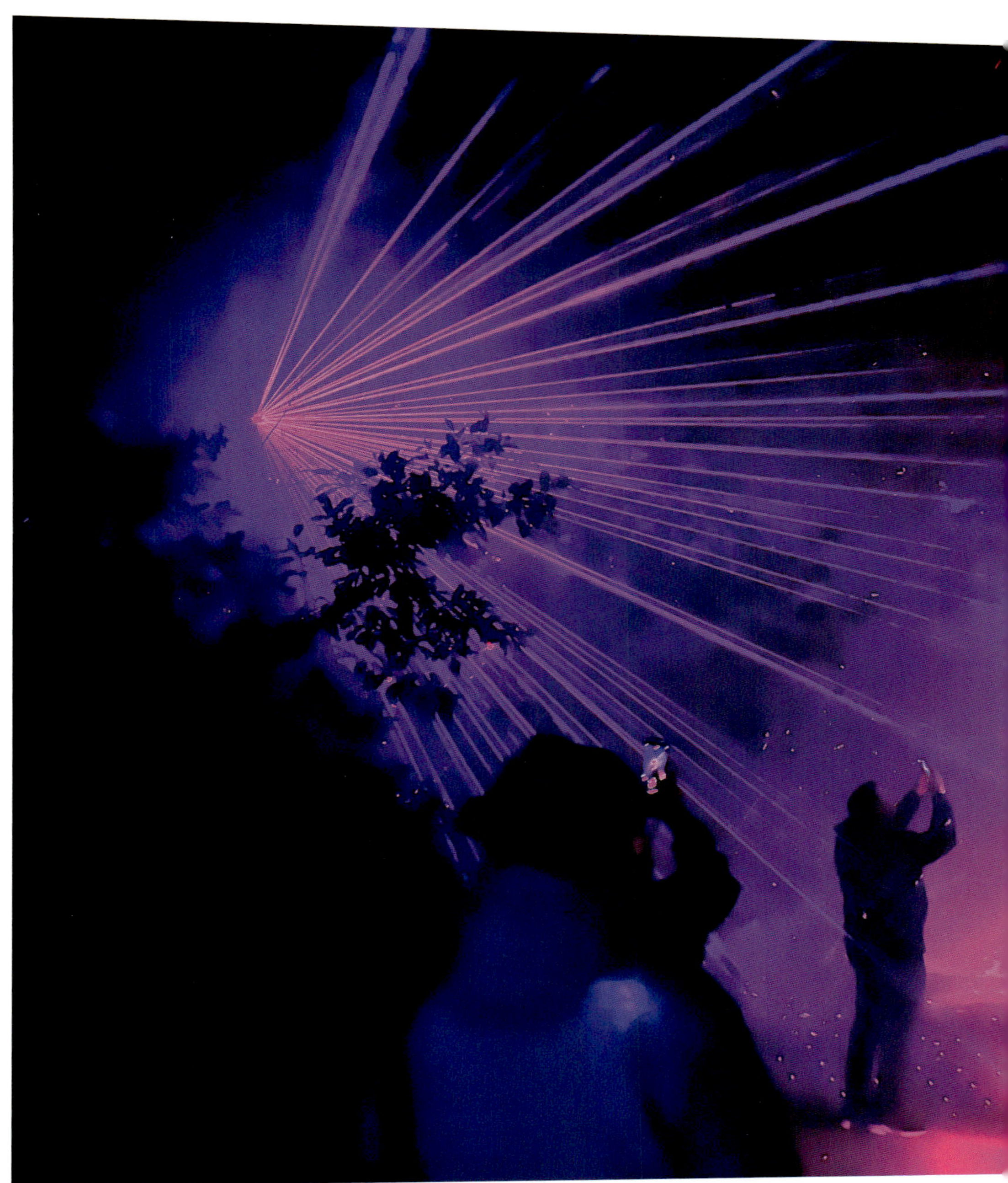

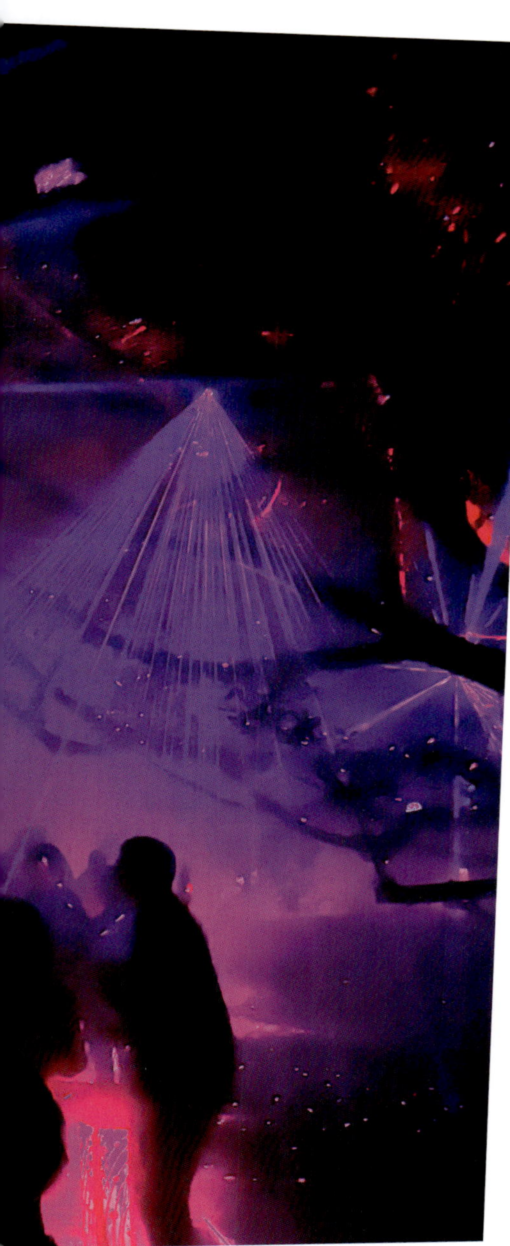

Playing in *Astra Lumina*, South Coast Botanic Garden, Palos Verdes Estates, Los Angeles, CA. Photo by Margaret Kerrison

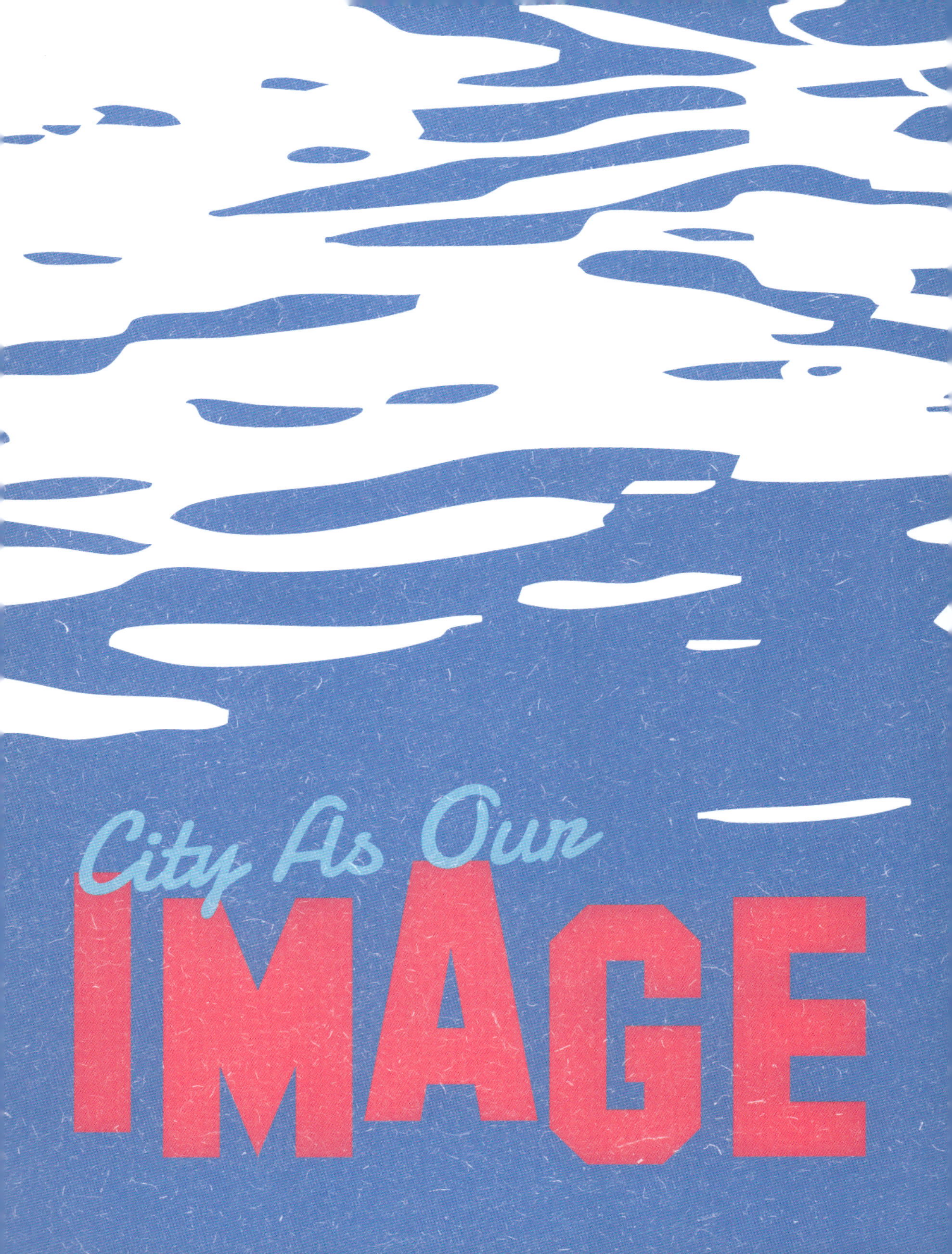
City As Our
IMAGE

"A place belongs forever to whoever claims it hardest, remembers it most obsessively, wrenches it from itself, shapes it, renders it, loves it so radically that he remakes it in his image."

Joan Didion,
The White Album (1979)

Los Angeles is not a city in the traditional sense. It is a sandbox. A sprawling, sun-soaked expanse of contradictions and possibilities. Unlike cities built on rigid foundations of tradition and legacy, LA has no such anchors. Its identity is fluid, unmoored, and for that very reason, liberating. Here, there are no rules—only tools. And for those who dare to pick them up, the city offers an infinite canvas on which to play, dream, and create.

On a flight into Los Angeles, I struck up a conversation with a longtime resident. We shared stories of how people back in Boston warned us off, convinced we'd be crawling back in no time. She smiled and said, almost conspiratorially, "Don't tell anyone how it really is over here. Let's keep it our secret." It wasn't just a joke—it was a quiet acknowledgment of the city's strange magic, the kind that only reveals itself to those willing to see past the smog, the chaos, the clichés.

LA is often misunderstood. Outsiders arrive searching for a blueprint, a path, some well-trodden route to success or fulfillment. But they quickly discover that no such map exists. It will never exist. Instead, they find fragments—scattered across neighborhoods and industries: a forgotten café in a rundown block, a closed down theater, a dusty backlot waiting for a scene that has not yet been written. The city speaks not in answers, but in questions and invitations: What will you create? What will you imagine? What will you do next?

This is a city made not by its infrastructure but by its collective imagination. Directors, designers, tinkerers, rebels, misfits—those who arrive as transplants, wide-eyed and unsure—soon learn that the only way to truly belong is to engage. Spectatorship is temporary. Participation is mandatory. Those who pick up the tools—be it a camera, a pen, a paintbrush, a microphone, or simply an unshakable idea—begin to shape not only their own futures, but the very fabric of the city itself. Together, they reimagine the city through their self-expression, one voice at a time.

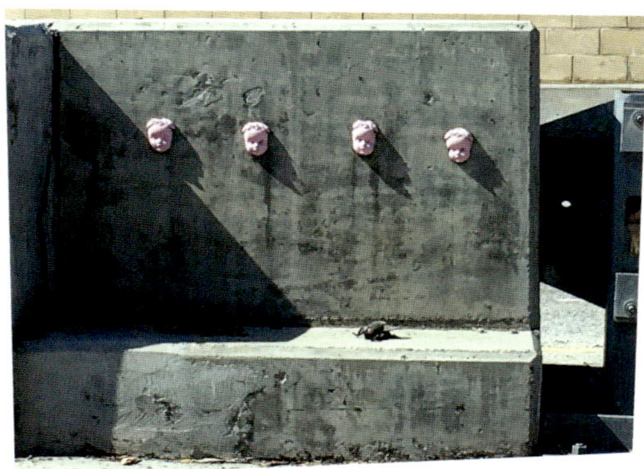

Street art found in Burbank, CA.
Photo by Margaret Kerrison

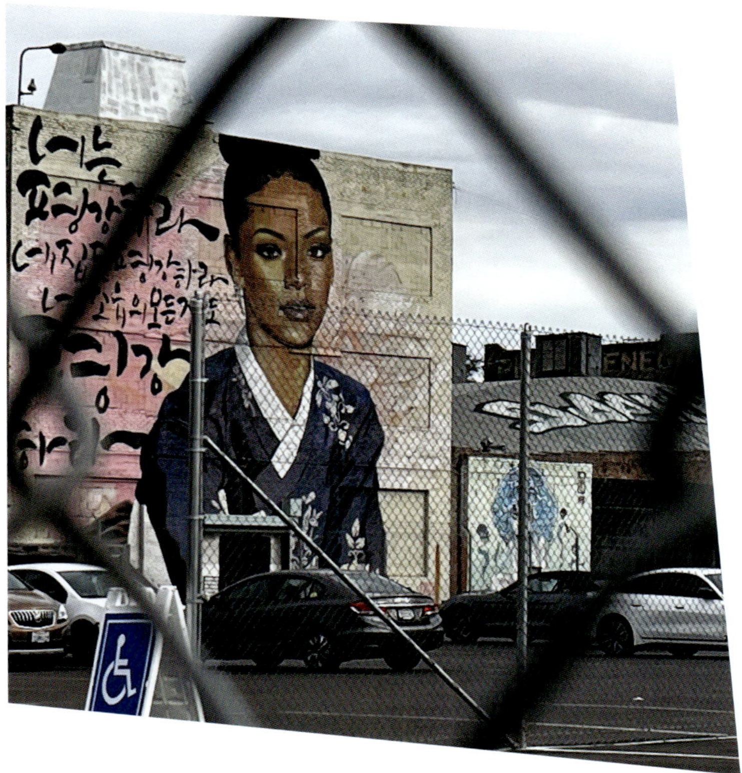

Graffiti in Downtown LA.
Photo by Margaret Kerrison

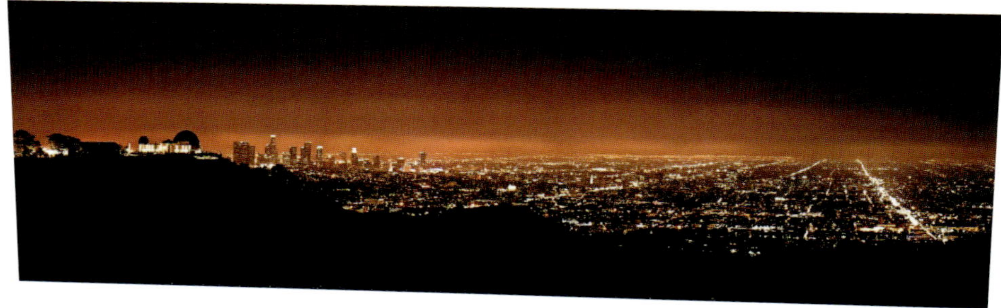

Dusk over Los Angeles, CA.
Photo by Foster Kerrison

There is a paradox to Los Angeles. It is indifferent—aloof, even—yet utterly open. It makes no promises. It does not coddle. But it rewards resilience, audacity, and invention. It doesn't play favorites, but it favors the bold. To thrive here is not to master the city, but to dance with it—to embrace its constant reinvention as your own.

In LA, your role is not cast for you. It must be claimed. The city asks: What do you want to build? What story do you want to tell? And more importantly: Are you willing to play, to fail, to iterate, to dream out loud with no safety net? For those who answer yes, the sandbox becomes sacred ground. A place where identity is not inherited, but imagined, and hopefully realized.

And so, the city becomes a mirror of its makers. Each wave of creatives leaves a mark—sometimes indelible, sometimes fleeting—but always contributing to the kaleidoscopic reinvention of this strange, elusive metropolis. Los Angeles is not a city that becomes; it is a city that is always becoming. And so we, too, are in a constant state of becoming.

This is the power of play. Not frivolous, but fundamental. Not directionless, but driven by purpose unbound by convention. In this city, to play is to dream, to build, to shape, to reimagine, to participate in. And those who choose to play do not merely find a place—they create one.

It poses a single question: *Do you want to play with us?*

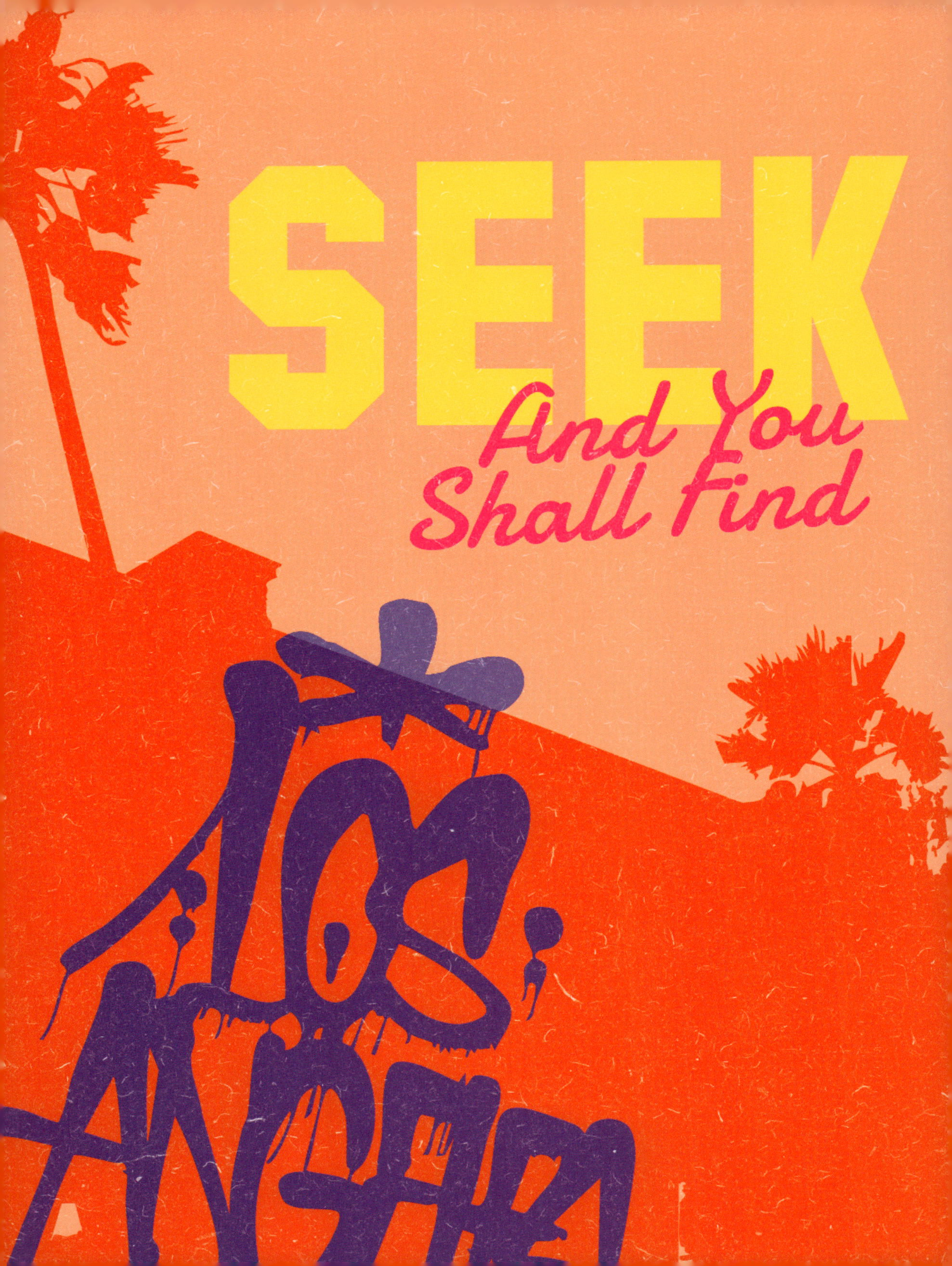
SEEK
And You Shall Find

When I first moved to Los Angeles, I didn't realize I was beginning a lifelong conversation—with a city, with its stories, with the spaces that hold both memory, possibility, and imagination. What I've come to understand over the years is that this city has a curious kind of magic: the kind that reveals itself slowly, in layers, through moments of unexpected beauty and discovery, for those who are curious enough to seek it. Everyone has their favorite locations, but I find myself constantly drawn to places where thoughtful design meets unexpected discovery, where a space doesn't just serve a function but tells a story—sometimes one you didn't even know you were seeking.

These are the places where structure offers moments of spontaneity, where the built environment coexists seamlessly with the unpredictable rhythm of life. They're not just landmarks or attractions—they're experiences. Invitations. Portals into our imagination, which quickly become rituals in our everyday lives.

Urban Spaces That Invite and Immerse

Take the Huntington Library. I remember my first visit like a dream unfolding in chapters. I wandered the gardens without a map, letting my feet lead the way. One moment I was in the beauty of the Rose Garden, the next, lost in the tranquil quiet of the Japanese Garden, and immersed in the otherworldly flora of the Desert Garden. It was like walking through living poetry, thoughtfully curated. Then I stumbled into the Children's Garden—not as a child, but as someone seeking a moment of lightness. It offered more than I expected: playful fountains, secret tunnels, tiny doorways carved into hedges.

Inside the library, I found old manuscripts that made me feel insignificant—in the best way. Like I was witnessing great milestones in history. On another visit, I attended the Lunar New Year celebration—drums beating, lion dancers performing, lanterns swaying. One of my many cultures, vividly on display—a space where I'm seen and represented. For over two decades, I've been a consistent visitor, always discovering something new to see or do. I first came with my husband, and later, we brought our son. He loves it just as much as we do. That's what I love about the Huntington—it's never the same place twice. It evolves with the seasons, with its visitors, with you.

Then there's The Last Bookstore in Downtown LA, which feels less like a shop and more like stepping into a surreal world. For a year, I didn't even realize there was a second floor! I was already content getting lost in the books downstairs—until one day, I discovered an entire other area upstairs, filled with even more to explore. It's a place where curiosity becomes your compass. The tunnel made of books, the archways, the unexpected art galleries—all of it seems to say: keep going, there's more.

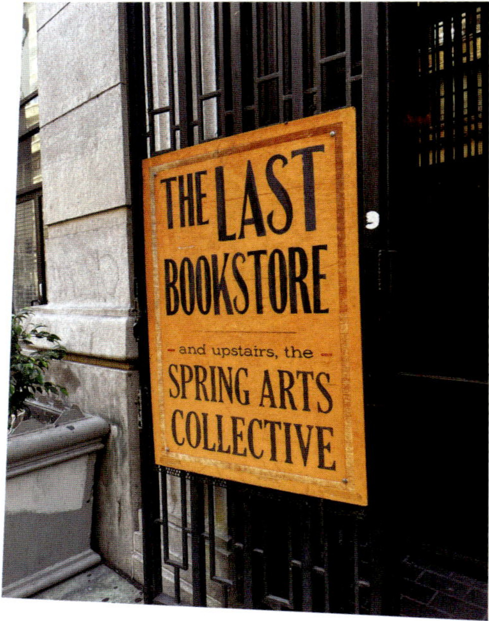

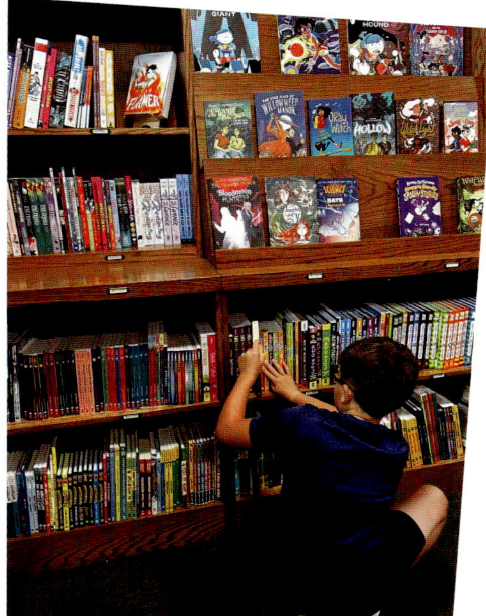

The Last Bookstore, Downtown Los Angeles.
Photo by Margaret Kerrison

But what truly defines that space is its sense of play. Books aren't arranged only by logic—they're arranged by theme and possibility. You can feel the designers' invitation: explore without expectation. And when you do, you often find something that feels like it was waiting for you all along. A new story to discover, a new world to explore.

A similar feeling lives at Hauser & Wirth in the Arts District. I've gone for the exhibitions, yes—but I've stayed for the sense of community, the garden tucked behind the gallery, and the chicken coop that makes you forget, for a moment, that you're in the heart of an industrial neighborhood. Many times, I've wandered into artist exhibits I hadn't planned on attending. Other times, I end up in the bookstore, flipping through books I'd never otherwise pick up. The restaurant, Manuela, spills into the community's creative energy. There's history all around, as the space was once a flour mill. You see the visual cues of what came before, and you can't help but feel like you're in the past, present, and future all at once.

Just down the road, you'll find yourself at Santa Fe One—a tiny universe of its own, with boutique shops and the quiet haven of Hennessey + Ingalls, a bookstore that invites you to linger and fall in love with the idea of architecture all over again. A short stroll from there, Little Tokyo opens like a portal, promising to transport you into a Japan-themed town. It's another place where the buzz and energy of a community converge. Beyond the shops and restaurants, there are street musicians, children playing, and cosplay-wearing teenagers, all eager to promenade through this vibrant setting. We may be far from Japan, but the history, context, and community here bring us closer to it.

Close to home, Magnolia Park offers a welcome respite from my day-to-day work. Nearly every day, I walk down Magnolia Boulevard, visiting the small businesses that line the street. I wander through the thrift and vintage stores, noting every little change in their decor or merchandise—like subtle shifts in the seasons. Occasionally, I chat with the shopkeepers, picking up on what's happening around Burbank and nurturing a sense of community.

Burbank feels small, intimate, family oriented, and a little quirky. Here, you can be whoever you want to be—and no one bats an eye. Take Carrie, the friendly owner of Hive & Hanger, who's also a beekeeper.

Inside her vintage store, she created a mini bee museum to share her love of bees.

Passion runs through this neighborhood, and we celebrate it in every way. From the Mystic Museum to Playclothes Vintage and the Cat Flea Vintage Market, people show up as their authentic selves—unapologetically—and it's inspiring to witness that every day.

Where Nature Becomes Narrative

And when I want to take a break from the urban scene, I retreat to the places where design softens into the landscape. The Getty Center is more than a museum—it's like origami unfolding in stone and light. The approach alone—a slow tram ride up the hill—feels ceremonial, like the city is preparing you to see something life-changing. For many, it is. Richard Meier's architecture frames the skyline like a painter choosing her canvas. Each terrace offers a new perspective, a new mood. I've gone for the art, of course. But the main draw is the view,

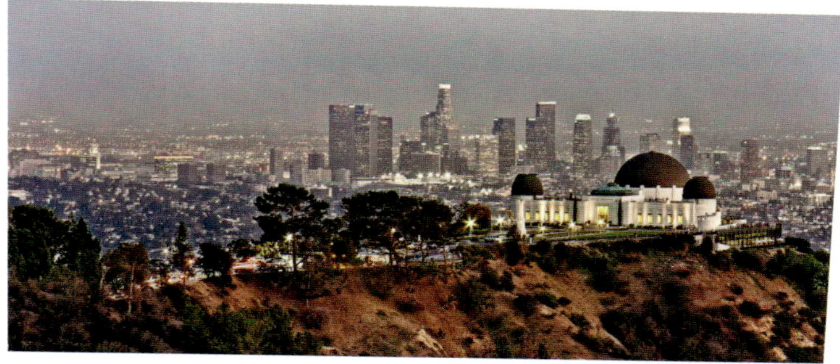

The Griffith Observatory.
Photo by Foster Kerrison

the gardens—and the city's light. The way it shifts throughout the day, casting shadows that make even the walkways feel alive. I've sat on the benches, watching both locals and tourists, feeling their excitement and inspiration. That, too, is part of the design. This is a place where you fall in love with the city—for the first time, and all over again.

And of course, there's the Griffith Observatory—what a special place. It feels like stepping onto the set of your own Hollywood movie. I've seen school groups marvel under the stars in the planetarium, families peer through the telescope, and tourists gawk at the city's sprawl from the rooftop. There's something sacred in that shared awe. I always feel like I'm stepping back in time, into a place of discovery—one that makes you feel small, in the best possible way. It reminds you of your place in the stars, of how we all come from the same origin. That no matter what worries you carry, they are insignificant in the grand scale of the universe. This place gives me perspective—a reminder of what truly matters in life.

But some of my favorite corners of Griffith Park are the ones I've discovered with my son. Travel Town is a place where childhood wonder comes alive among the old and miniature trains—climbing aboard, ringing the railroad crossing signal, pretending we're off on grand adventures. Every time we stepped into Travel Town with my then train-obsessed son, his heart would fill with joy and excitement, as if he were meeting all his best friends in one place. Now, when we return, I look at every corner of the place—each one holding a distinct memory: the time we hosted his birthday party, the many afternoons we spent at the old store location playing with the train table, the day we bumped into friends and picnicked together. It's a place filled with our most cherished memories.

Nearby, there's the Live Steamers Railroad Museum, where you can ride another even smaller scale miniature train and visit Walt Disney's Carolwood Barn. And then there's the carousel, with its hand-carved horses and old-time music that seems to spin you right out of the present. These places are so magical in their own way. We lose track of time there, moving between the past and imagination, and everywhere in between.

"The Happy Ones"

Tucked away in plain sight, Los Feliz is another personal favorite—one that neighborhood locals proudly claim as their own. Its name, literally translated from Spanish as "The Happy Ones," hints at the unique, laid-back charm that runs through its streets. Over the years, the area has evolved into one of LA's most storied and eclectic corners.

Walkable and full of character, Los Feliz offers more than just cozy cafés and indie bookstores. Its architectural landscape is a patchwork of eras and styles—from iconic mid-century modern homes to whimsical storybook-style houses and Frank Lloyd Wright's Mayan Revival masterpiece, the Hollyhock House, located within Barnsdall Art Park. Here, history and imagination linger on every corner. You'll find historic apartment buildings with ornate facades, quirky bungalow courts, and the occasional oddly shaped structure that feels plucked from a movie set.

I've spent hours browsing through racks of vintage clothes, picking out a new book to fall in love with at Skylight Bookstore, watching a friend's play at the Skylight Theatre Company, and lunching with friends on a broad mix of cuisines—from Japanese handrolls to tacos and escargot. I love walking over to Wacko Soap Plant to check out the free local art gallery and pick up a gift in the curiously curated store, which offers everything from witchcraft books to kawaii mementos. Los Feliz isn't just a neighborhood—it's a vibe, a small world within the sprawl, where every type of Angeleno is welcome. It's a microcosm of what LA truly is.

The City as Storyteller

Los Angeles isn't always easy, especially for visitors and newcomers. It sprawls. It hides. It makes you search. But that's part of its brilliance. Its best stories are not laid out for all to see—they're tucked into corners, hidden from the masses, whispered among locals, layered into its landscapes. The places I love most in this city are the ones that blur the line between what's designed and what's discovered. They are spaces that invite us not only to look, but to linger. To lose ourselves. To find ourselves anew.

These places reward those who take the time to seek them out. It takes patience to uncover all the special nooks and crannies of the city. They're there, waiting to be discovered by the next unsuspecting passerby—like rare jewels hidden in plain sight.

As a designer, I believe in the power of narrative placemaking. But as a human being, I believe even more in the spaces that surprise us, that make us feel something we didn't expect. That's what Los Angeles offers—when you let it. Not just destinations, but moments. Not just architecture, but meaning.

And for those who seek them, those moments are everywhere. You just have to keep wandering.

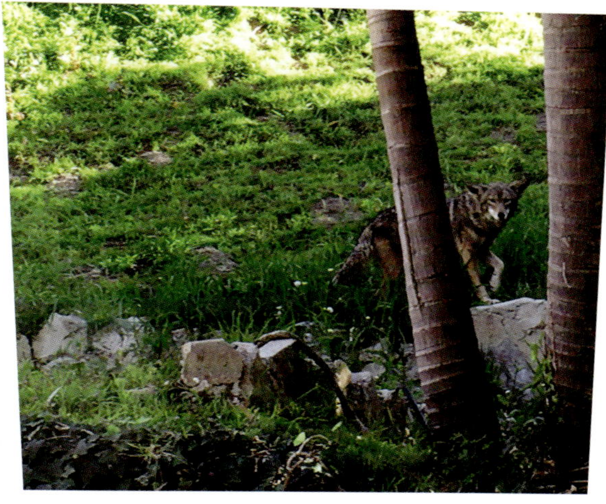

Coyote spotted wandering in Griffith Park, Los Angeles, CA. Photo by Margaret Kerrison

Thoughts On Wandering...

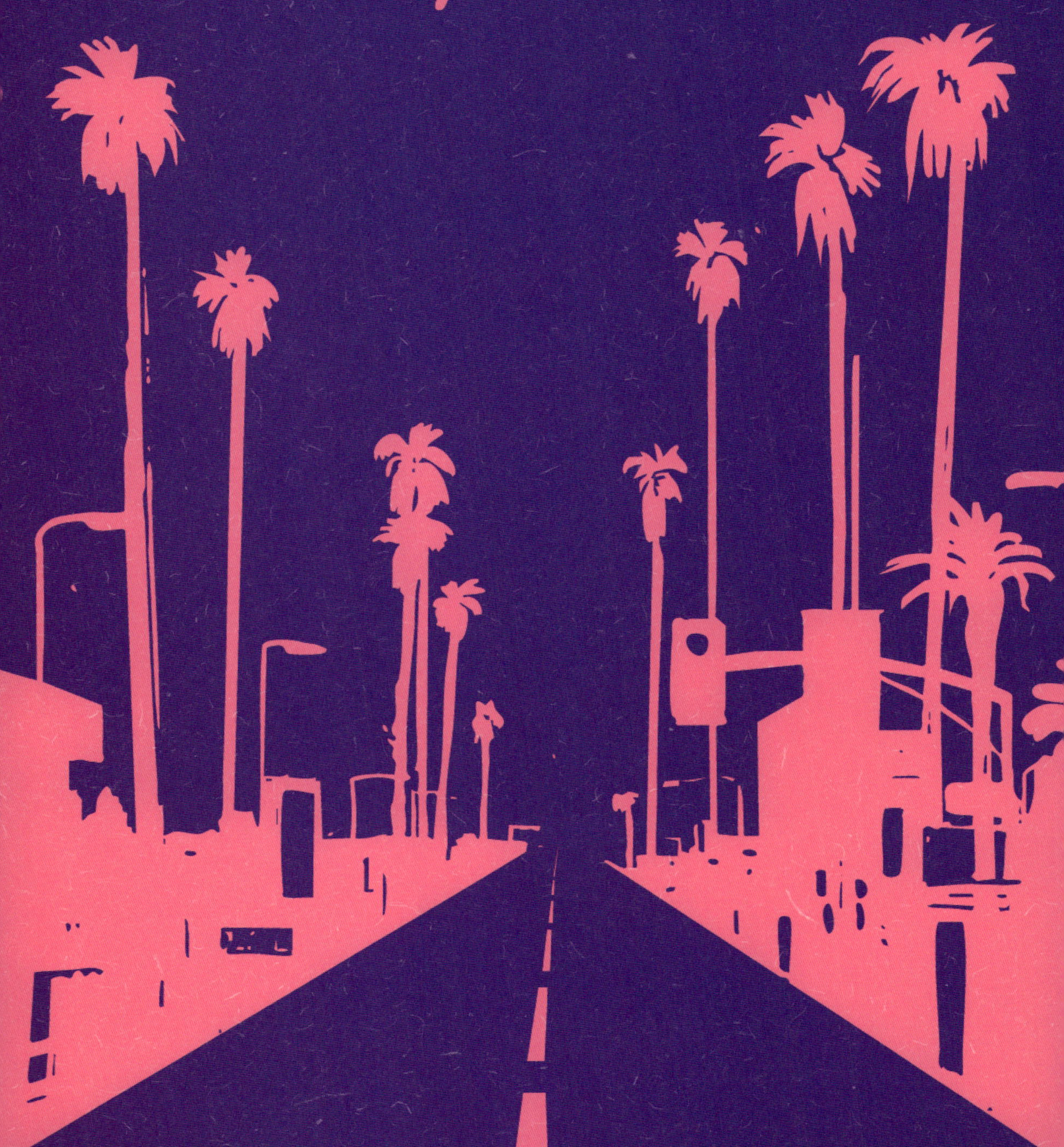

"A city is a language, a repository of possibilities, and walking is the act of speaking that language, of choosing from those possibilities."

Wanderlust: A History of Walking,
Rebecca Solnit

One of the questions I'm asked most often as a writer and creator is: "Where do you find your inspiration?"

There are many ways to answer. I could say I'm inspired by the world—by the work of other writers, designers, filmmakers, and artists. Their creativity often sparks my own.

But my real answer is simpler, and more tangible: I wander.

When I wander, I reconnect with a sense of energy, curiosity, and inspiration that I can't find anywhere else. For a long time, I didn't realize there was a word for what I was already doing.

Wandering through a city, quietly observing its people and rhythms, is hardly a new idea. The term *flâneur*—popularized by nineteenth-century French poet Charles Baudelaire—likely comes from the Old Norse *flana*, meaning "to wander without purpose."

But what looks like aimlessness on the outside can be deeply intentional on the inside.

When you train your mind to receive rather than simply consume, you start to see differently. You begin connecting dots others miss. You notice patterns, assemble fragments, and generate insights that feel surprising, even to you. You become more observant—a vital skill for any creative or designer.

Observation fuels originality. Watching the world—its people, its systems, its odd details—offers raw material for making things that resonate. Often, it gives rise to ideas the world didn't know it needed.

Wandering, though, takes time—and practice. Many people say they can't afford to wander. But I believe we can make time, if we choose to prioritize it. I often skip social plans to protect my sacred solo wandering time. It's as essential to me as sleep or nourishment. It's how I refuel—mentally, emotionally, and even physically.

Wandering isn't wasting time; it's *making* time—for thought, for noticing, for being present. I walk every day. On days I don't—days spent at a desk, tethered to screens—I feel unmoored. There's a reason we need to move, breathe, and engage with the world around us. It resets us. It returns us to ourselves.

"What the flâneurs are doing is looking. They are opening their eyes and ears to the scene around them. They are not treating the street like an obstacle course to be negotiated. They are opening themselves up to it ... They relish what is up to date, loving the trendy." — Alain de Botton, "A Good Idea from Charles Baudelaire," *US Modernist* (2006)

The flâneur, first introduced by Baudelaire in *The Painter of Modern Life* (1863), is the archetype of the sophisticated urban wanderer—an observer who finds meaning in the motion of crowds and the texture of city life. This figure, both engaged and aloof, has become iconic in modern literature and culture.

Originally meaning "man of leisure," the flâneur was later reimagined by Walter Benjamin as a thoughtful drifter—an ambivalent participant in modernity. More recently, writers like Lauren Elkin have expanded the concept to include flâneuses: women who explore cities with curiosity, purpose, and creative agency.

The flâneur observes without intruding—blending into the crowd while paying close attention to its subtleties. They don't walk for the sake of arriving; they walk to discover. Their power lies in this balance of detachment and immersion, turning the everyday into something quietly extraordinary.

"For Baudelaire, the intrusions he experienced in the city became images in his poems. Walking the streets and slipping into the 'ebb and flow of the multitudes,' he picked up urban detritus and wove it into his poetry ... A rip in the veil of the crowd let him see through the city's scrim into poetic moments." — Frances McCue, "Flâneur: City Wanderer," *US Modernist* (2006)

Many celebrated writers and artists have embodied the spirit of the flâneur, attuned to the subtle rhythms of city life. Designers, too, have embraced this ethos of observation and learning from their surroundings. Among them, Charles and Ray Eames, the visionary American duo, stood out as keen observers of the world. Their designs reflected a profound understanding of human behavior and culture, shaped by a broad, interdisciplinary curiosity—spanning architecture, furniture, film, photography, and exhibitions—all of which informed and enriched one another.

Like flâneurs, the Eameses valued experimentation and playful exploration. They collaborated widely, drew inspiration from diverse people and places, and seamlessly incorporated cultural influences into their work. Their openness to the world mirrored the flâneur's sociability and engagement with the everyday poetry of urban life.

In contrast, yet equally reflective of the urban experience, is the work of Edward Hopper—one of my favorite artists. His paintings often capture the quiet solitude of city living, portraying isolated figures suspended in moments of introspection. In iconic works like *Nighthawks* and *Automat*, people appear lost in thought, disconnected from their surroundings. Yet for me, these scenes evoke calm rather than loneliness—reflecting a kind of inner peace amid external chaos. The city is not something separate from myself; it is an extension of who I am. Together, we belong.

This relationship between self and city gained further depth in the mid-twentieth century through the work of French Marxist theorist Guy Debord. As a founder of the Situationist International, Debord introduced the concept of psychogeography—the study of how urban environments shape our emotions and behaviors. In his 1955 essay "Introduction to a Critique of Urban Geography," he outlined the practice of the *dérive*: aimless drifting through city streets to uncover their psychological effects.

Here, the flâneur becomes a psychogeographer—wandering not with a destination in mind, but with the intention of feeling and mapping the city's emotional contours. In doing so, they reveal hidden stories embedded in buildings, streets, and parks. These spaces are not neutral; they carry the imprints of history, culture, and human presence, shaping how the city is experienced and understood.

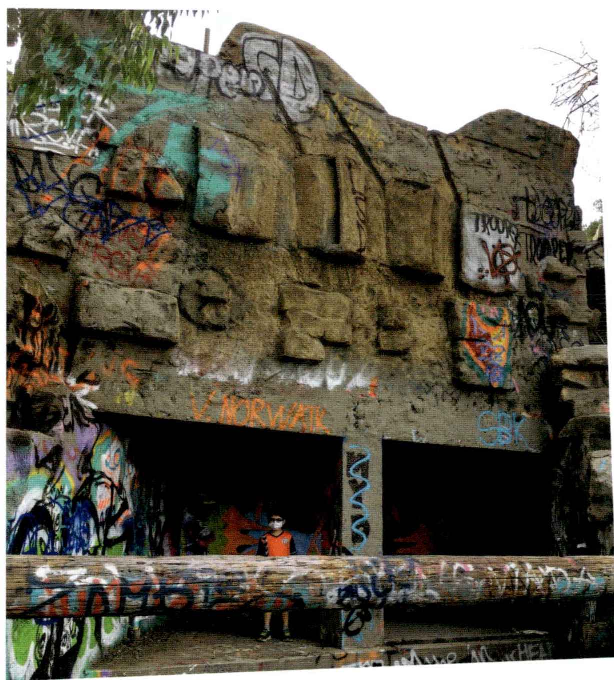

Exploring the Old Los Angeles Zoo, Griffith Park.
Photo by Margaret Kerrison

Imagine cities designed for emotional resonance, not just functionality. What if every space aimed to evoke positive feelings—joy, tranquility, connection—rather than stress or isolation? If architects and planners prioritized emotional impact, they could transform how we live and interact.

I wander every day. I make time to roam without purpose through the neighborhoods I've known—from my childhood in Singapore, to my college days in Boston, to my adult life in Los Angeles. Wandering is a constant in a changing life. I worry that many have lost the art of wandering, believing they lack leisure time. Yet, I argue it is essential—especially for creative thinkers and problem solvers.

Growing up, my family often went *jalan jalan*—literally "to stroll" in Bahasa Indonesia—whether to shopping centers, indoor markets, and other recreation areas. It was more than walking; it was how I learned about life outside my family, observing how others lived and interacted. It was my window to a fascinating world beyond me, teaching me that I was a small part of something bigger.

Maybe my love of wandering comes from growing up in Singapore—one of the best cities to wander in. A place where history and modernity live side by side, often within the same block. Where nature and urban life coexist in an ecosystem designed with people in mind.

When I moved to the US for college, I didn't plan to return to Singapore. Our childhood home was gone, and my parents had moved back to Indonesia—where I was born, but never truly felt at home. I had to quickly adapt to each new city I lived in. Wandering, perhaps, became my way of connecting to the world on my own terms—without the pressure to belong.

Like many multicultural immigrants, I've come to accept that my sense of belonging is fluid—rooted more in people and relationships than in place. The environment is where I find insight and inspiration. Over time, my wandering has evolved—from family outings to solo explorations, to wandering with friends and my own family. The act remains the same: observe and wander without purpose.

This is why, to this day, I find myself wandering through the cities where I live, work, and travel. Urban environments continue to inspire me—

they are dynamic, accessible, and filled with anonymity, making them ideal for disappearing into the crowd. There's an energy to it: a sense of being swept up in the rush of life, carried along to unexpected and undiscovered places. Every new corner, every fleeting activity, sparks joy and curiosity—a little dopamine hit that urges me to keep exploring.

So wander—with open eyes and an open heart. Let your footsteps carry you through the overlooked and the everyday, where meaning often hides in plain sight. Wandering isn't a distraction or a detour—it's an invitation. To slow down. To notice. To feel. To connect with the world not through ownership or belonging, but through presence.

In wandering, we reclaim a quiet kind of freedom: the freedom to observe without expectation, to belong without boundaries. It's not just how we navigate cities—it's how we begin to see more clearly, imagine more boldly, and live more fully.

Los Angeles in the evening.
Photos by Foster Kerrison

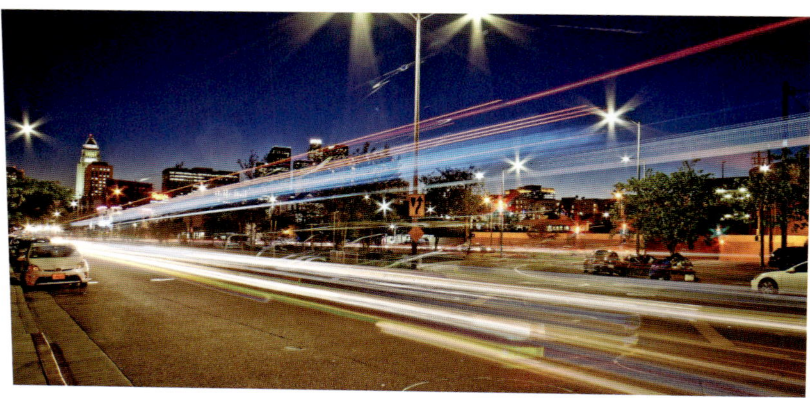

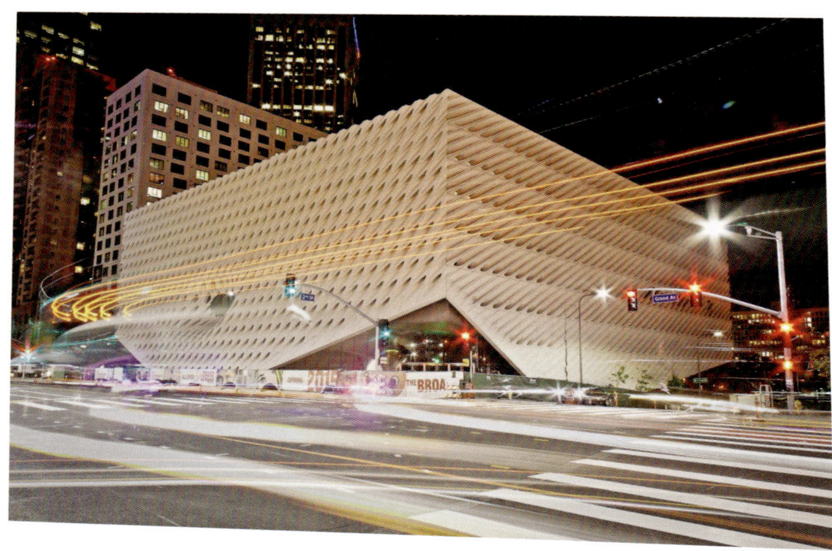
THE BROA

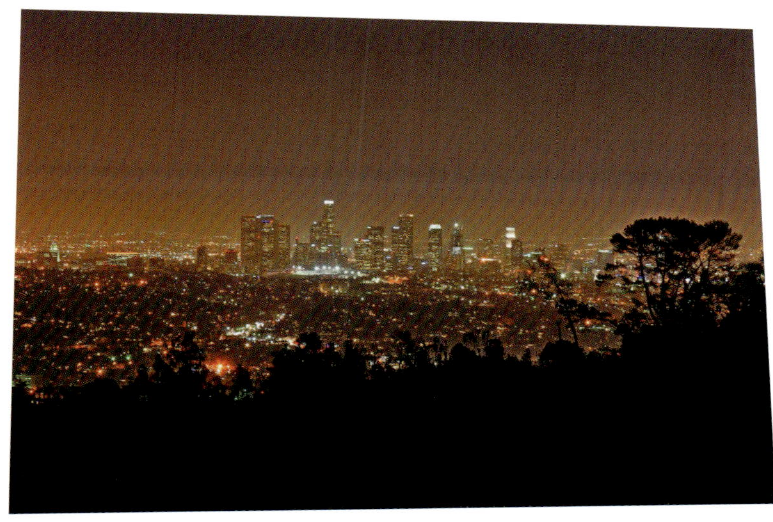

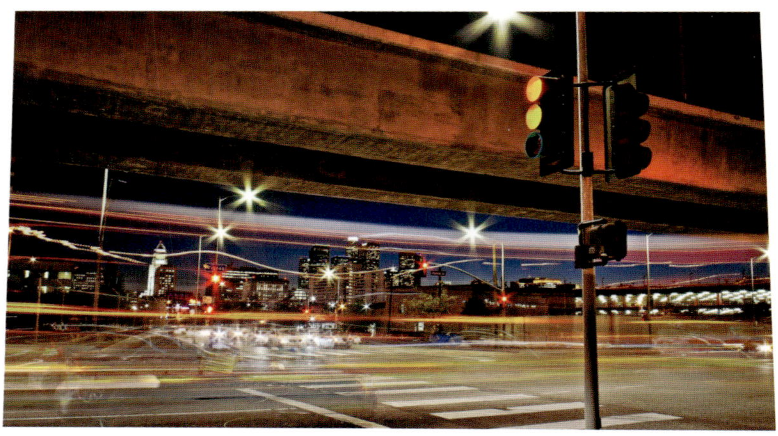

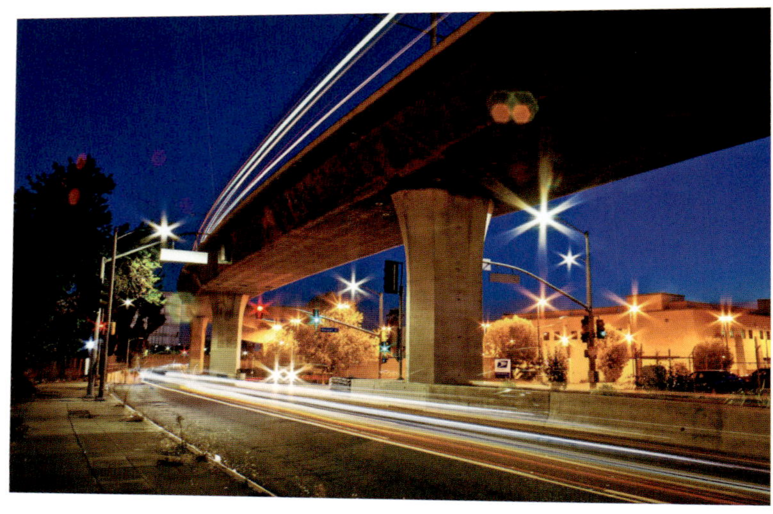

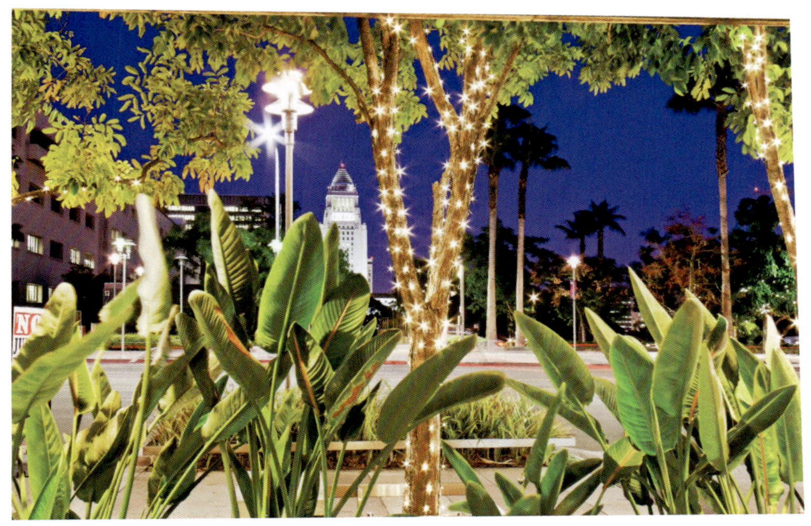

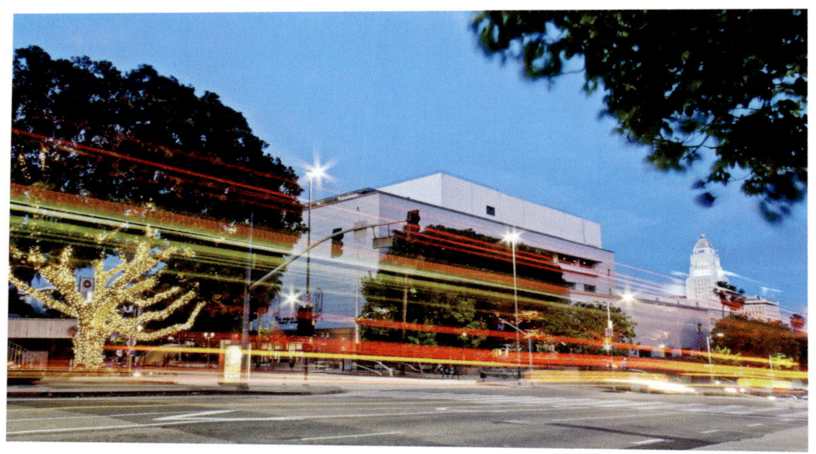

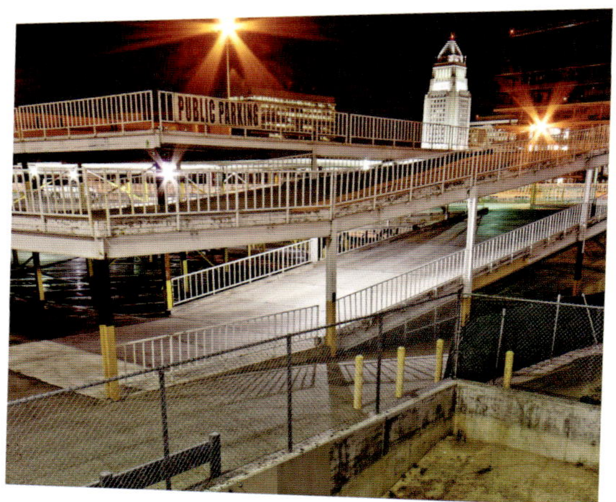
PUBLIC PARKING

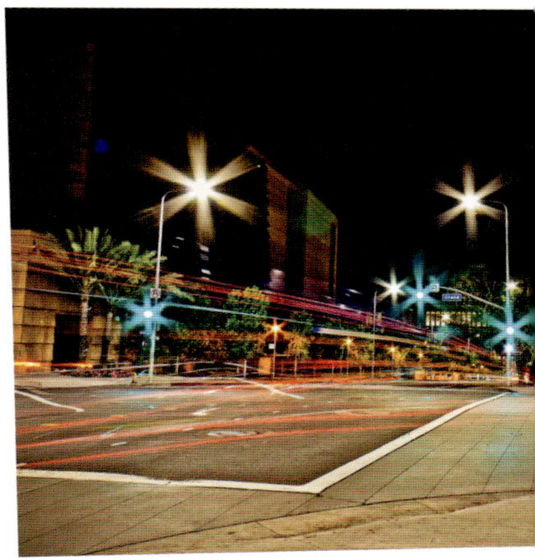

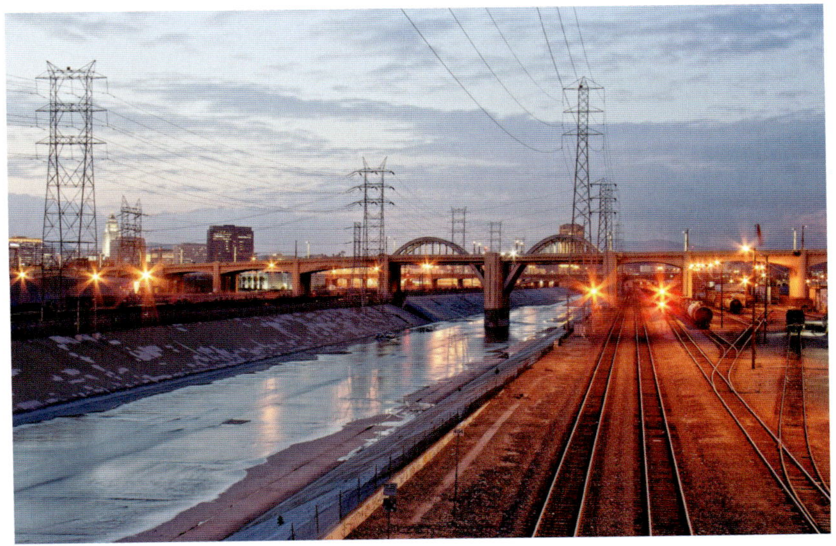

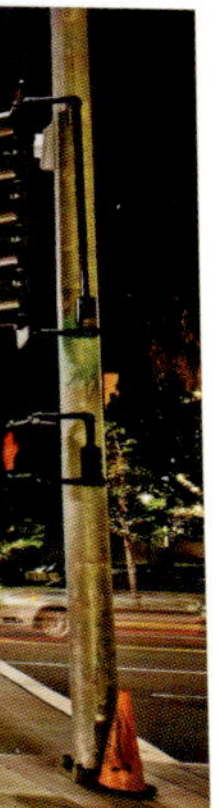

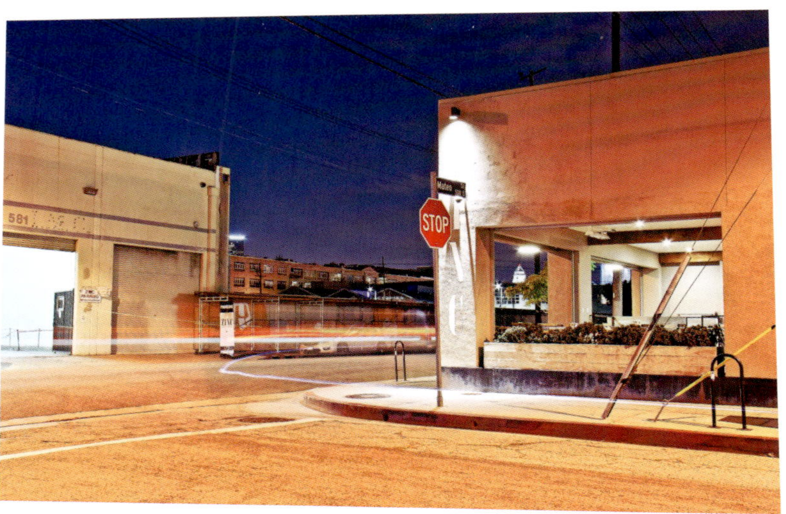
581
Mateo
STOP

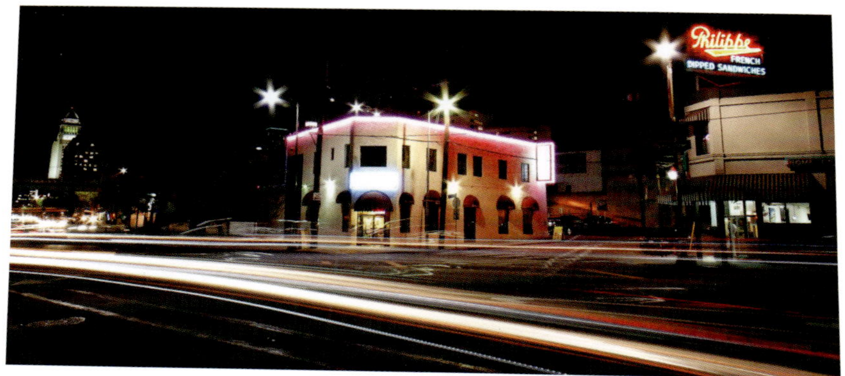
Philippe
FRENCH
DIPPED SANDWICHES

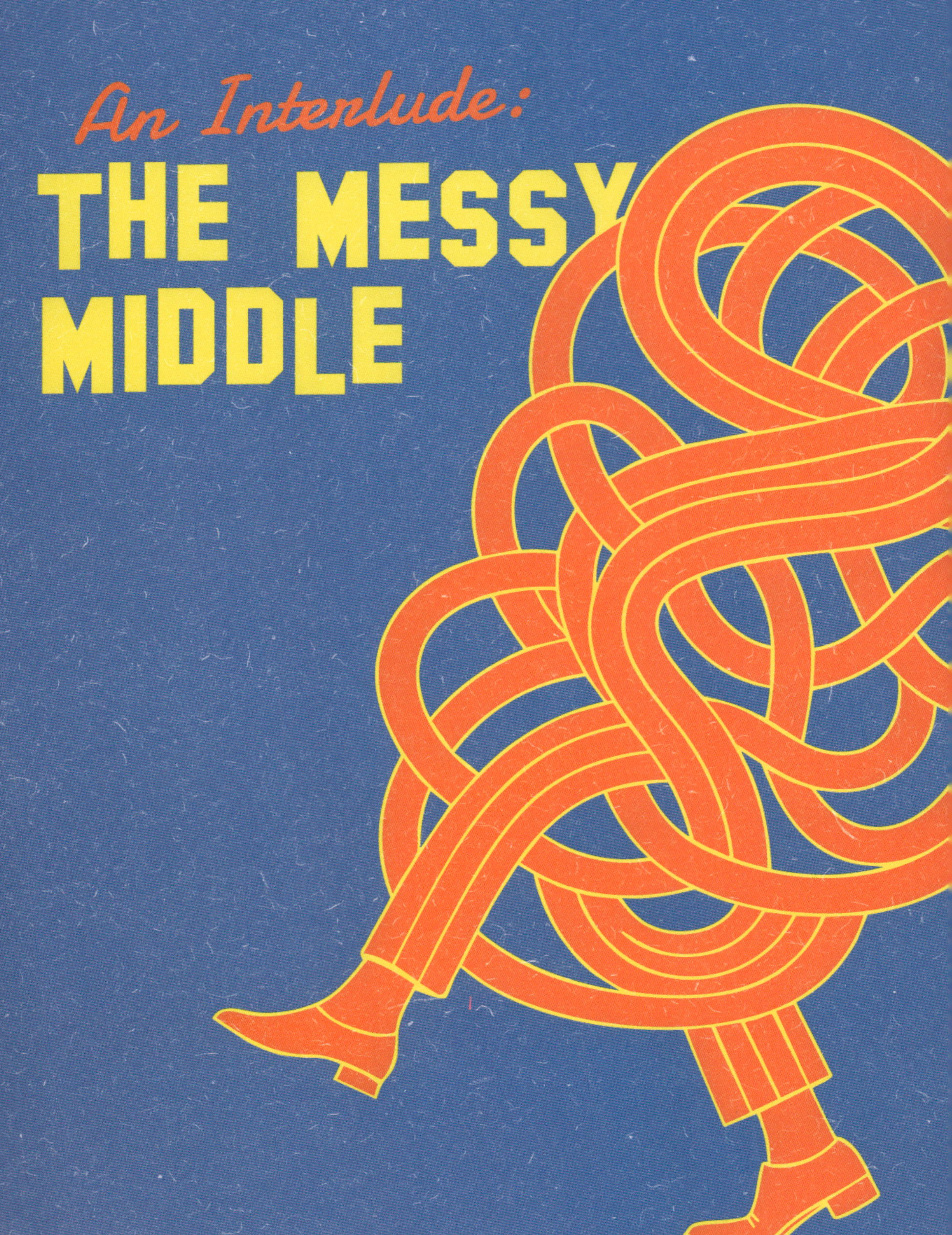
An Interlude:
THE MESSY MIDDLE

As creatives, we talk often about beginnings. The spark of a new idea. The thrill of a leap into something unknown. We celebrate the end too—the polished product, the celebratory opening, the finish line. But rarely do we speak honestly about the middle. The messy, uncertain, grueling, necessary middle. The part where most of us stay far longer than we expected. For the middle is the process. And you must love the process, the daily grind, in order to finish anything.

Maybe we avoid it because we don't want to acknowledge it. Maybe we fear being reminded of it. But the truth is, this stretch—this uncertain in-between—is the most important part of the creative journey. Can you endure the day-to-day, knowing that the only way out is through?

It is in this space—between the hopeful start and the hoped-for ending—that doubt creeps in, uninvited. I've come to see the messy middle not as a detour but as the path. It's the stretch where I find myself asking, over and over: Is this what I want? Is this still aligned with who I am and who I want to be? These are not indulgent questions; they are necessary ones. Especially when the work becomes hard, the progress slow, and the validation from others scarce or nonexistent. When you're younger, the external validation comes fairly often from those around you. As you get older, as you get into the messy middle of life, the validation has to come from within. No one prepares you for that.

The middle is where most of our story happens. It's where we confront ourselves. Where we begin to distinguish between the dreams we held on for too long and the ones we were born to follow. There's a kind of quiet rebellion in asking, "Am I pursuing something that matters to me, and not just to others?" That question alone can cut through the noise.

So it's fitting—perfect, even—that this short essay sits in the middle of this book. Right here, halfway through, is a pause. A breath. A moment to look around and ask: What is truly important to me right now? I am in the middle of writing, in the middle of creating, and yes, in the middle of life. Middle age has a way of stripping away the pretense. It invites reflection, sometimes insistently: Where am I, and where am I going?

I used to believe that by now I would have clarity. Instead, I have deeper questions. But they are richer, fuller, more honest. I've come to understand that I don't need to have all the answers. I just need to ask the right questions—and keep asking them.

Whether I am building my own project or contributing to someone else's vision, I ask: Does this align with my values? Does this reflect the kind of world I want to help create? If the answer is yes, then I can get up and do it again tomorrow—not out of obligation, but out of devotion. That is what the messy middle teaches me: to keep choosing what matters, even when the path is unclear.

And in this process, I am slowly learning to let go of who I used to be and to never be afraid of becoming someone else. Someone who has grown and evolved into another version of me. To accept that it may not align with someone's idea of me. To defy their expectations and disappoint many who watch near and from afar. To always, always listen to my instinct and curiosity, no matter where it takes me.

This is the part of the story where we decide what's worth carrying forward—and what we can finally let go. It's not the end, and it's not the beginning. It's the becoming.

So I'll stay in it. Not forever, not blindly, but intentionally. I will keep asking:

Is this my path?

Is this helping me become more of who I already am?

Am I excited to rise and do it again tomorrow?

Because when the answer is yes—even on the messy days—I know I am exactly where I need to be.

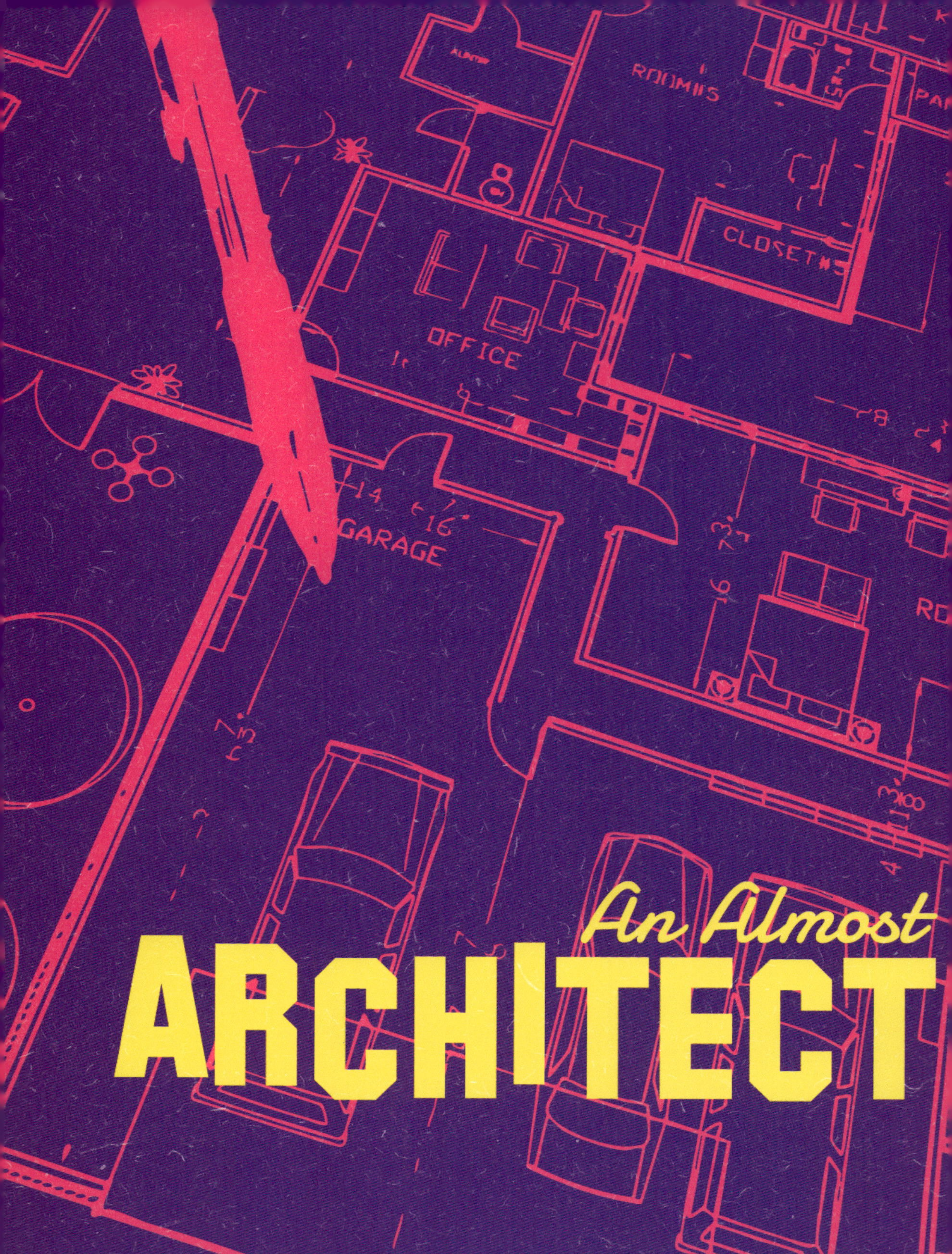

ROOM #5
CLOSET #5
OFFICE
GARAGE
An Almost
ARCHITECT

I couldn't wait to leave college—not because I didn't enjoy learning, but because I was eager to start the next chapter of my life, whatever form it might take. After graduating from Tufts University in three years with a BA in International Relations, I found myself at a curious crossroads. I was twenty years old—barely an adult by most standards—and though I held the degree, I had no clear sense of what to do next. Everyone expected me to dive headfirst into a promising career or apply to graduate school right away. But I wasn't ready.

Instead, I rented a charming brownstone apartment on Marlborough Street, just a few blocks from the bustle of Newbury Street in Boston. The building was classic New England—ivy-covered, brick-lined, and elegant in that understated way that makes you feel like you've stepped into a storybook. I hoped the city might help me find my footing. Maybe, if I stayed still long enough, the answer would come.

That year, I worked as a project administrator for the Harvard-MIT Retinal Implant project at the Massachusetts Eye and Ear Infirmary. I spent my days transcribing medical assessments, compiling data, and helping write grants for work that I didn't always understand. Important work, yes—but also a far cry from what I had imagined my early twenties would look like. Still, I kept at it, telling myself I was gaining experience. But truthfully, I was drifting, unsure of where I fit in a world that suddenly felt too big.

Eventually, I scaled back to part-time work. I needed space—mental, emotional, and creative space—to pause and breathe. To reflect. Looking back now, I realize that year was my unofficial "gap year." A necessary break between the intensity of academia and the unknown future. A precious, in-between time where I could explore the question that would shape the rest of my life: Who was I becoming? What kind of life did I want to build? And more importantly, what would it mean to live on my own terms?

I invited my sister to move in with me. We were two young women, recent college graduates and immigrants from Singapore, both searching for something but not quite sure what. That tiny one-bedroom on the top floor became our sanctuary. The rent was $1,450 a month—steep at the time—but we didn't care. The location was everything. The "bedroom" was so small that two twin beds barely fit, and opening the door cut the room in two. It was comically cramped, but we didn't mind. We laughed about it. It was ours.

A brownstone in the Back Bay was a dream, and we were living it. We were just blocks from the Charles River and an easy stroll to Boston Common. The T could take us anywhere, and everything else was walkable. I didn't own a car for six of the eight years I eventually spent in Boston—and I loved that. There was freedom in that kind of urban living. We'd walk to dinner, to bookstores and Tower Records, to tiny shops tucked between brownstones. There were Asian and Italian restaurants everywhere, and we made it a point to try as many as possible. Our favorite was this little Japanese place that served comforting home-cooked meals for cheap. We went there at least twice a week. It became our kitchen by default.

And yes, our kitchenette was laughable. We couldn't open the oven door all the way without it smacking into the wall. We didn't cook—not because of the space (though it certainly didn't help)—but because we had never really learned how. Cooking just wasn't part of our upbringing. We tried twice: once to make beef and broccoli with rice, which came out overcooked and overseasoned, and another time when I attempted to impress my boyfriend by making packet-ready beef *rendang*. It was inedible. My sister and I quickly decided to leave the cooking to the professionals.

In the evenings, I'd take long, meandering walks. I loved how the city transformed at dusk—how the lights cast a soft glow against the old brick buildings. One of my favorite stops was the Brutalist-style building at 320 Newbury Street: the Boston Architectural College—BAC. I'd slip into the lobby, pretending I belonged, and quietly admired the student work displayed on the walls. I was mesmerized. I immersed myself in a lifelong childhood curiosity: could I be an architect too?

There was something deeply captivating about the idea of creating spaces—shaping environments where people lived, worked, and dreamed. I loved the precision and the poetry of architecture. The way a simple sketch could become something real. Something lasting. Something that stood. Something to be shared.

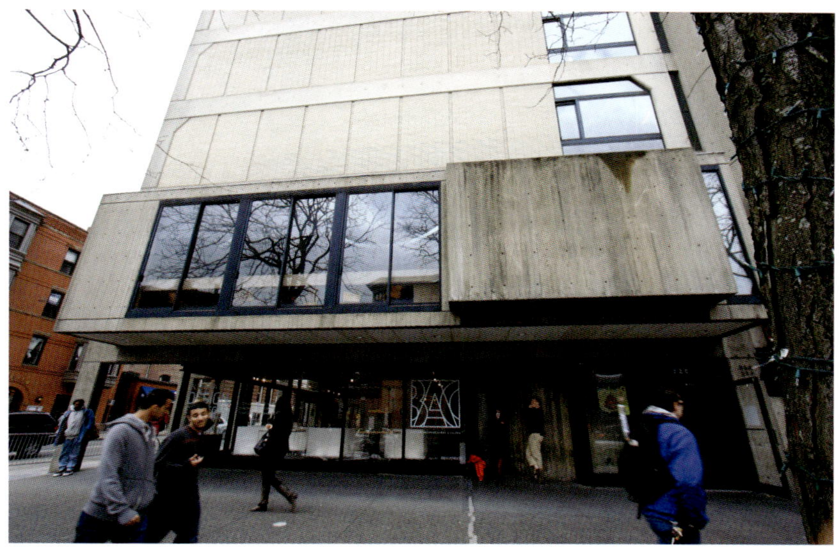

A building used by the Boston Architectural College, photographed during the "Wikipedia Takes Boston" scavenger hunt on April 17, 2011.
Photo by Cryptic C62. CC BY-SA 3.0

After several months, I finally applied. The BAC had a unique work-study program: a rigorous seven-year journey that required students to work at an architectural firm while pursuing their studies. It wasn't for the faint of heart, but I was intrigued. The best part? Their open admissions policy. They were committed to diversity and to giving opportunities to people who might not otherwise have access to design education.

Getting in was the easy part—probably the smoothest admissions process of my life. I attended the open house. I listened intently. And when it ended, I stood outside the building for a moment. Seven years. That was a long time to commit to something I wasn't entirely sure about. The truth was, I wanted to build worlds, yes—but not as an architect. Not with blueprints and permits. My vision was different. Less defined. More fluid. I couldn't articulate my vision yet, but I was always drawn to storytelling, to entertainment and experiences, to the magic that happens when you create a place that exists as much in someone's imagination as it does in the real world.

So I didn't go back. Not because I wasn't capable, but because I knew in my bones that my path lay elsewhere. I didn't want a professional title to define me. I wanted to define myself. I wanted to make something no one had made before. I didn't have the vocabulary for it then—but I knew it when I felt it: a calling toward something uncharted, something exciting because it wasn't safe. That scared me. But it also lit a fire in me.

It would have been easier to pick a known path, to follow a template, to seek validation through conventional success. But that's not what I wanted. I wasn't looking for a roadmap. I wanted to draw my own. To carve out a space in this world that was uniquely mine, shaped by my values, my curiosity, my dreams, my intuition. It meant letting go of the need for approval, for clarity, for certainty. It meant learning to trust myself. To believe that I could create meaning and beauty in ways that hadn't been done before.

I didn't know where it would lead me. And that's the thing—when you're creating something new, you often don't. But that's where the magic is. In the uncertainty. In the exploration. In the quiet courage it takes to say, "This is who I am, even if no one else sees it yet." I wasn't interested in living someone else's life, following someone else's script. I wanted to write my own story. Page by page. Step by step. With heart, and with hope.

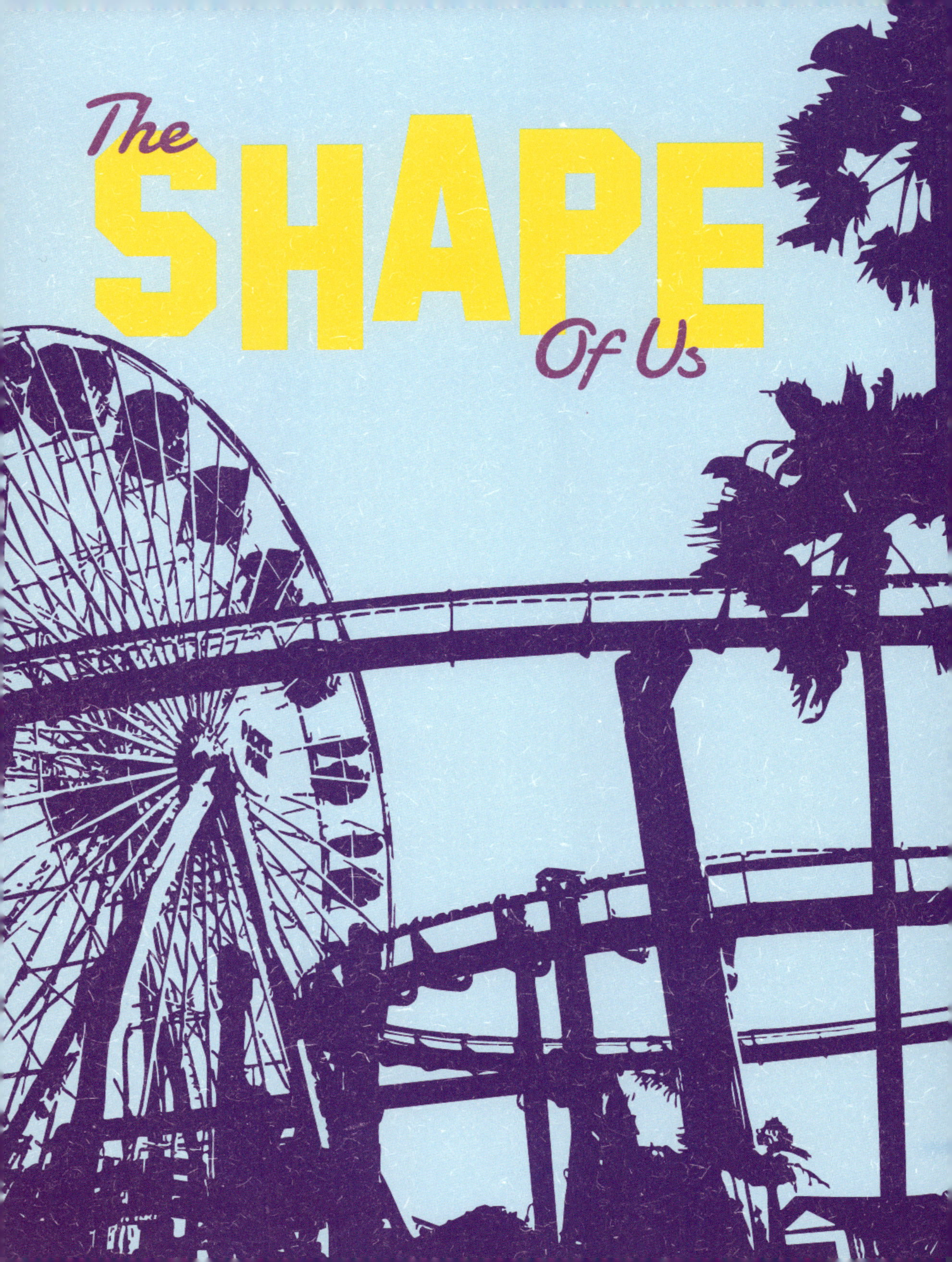
The
SHAPE
Of Us

I had a random thought one day. If I stripped away everything around me—the furniture, the walls, the objects I encounter daily—and focused solely on the actions my body performs and the routines I unconsciously follow, what would my life look like? Imagine your life as if a mime were acting it out. Remove all distractions and simply observe the motions. What are we doing? Would we even recognize one another's movements? Picture life as an improv game of "What are you doing?"

For instance, think of dialing a rotary phone if you were born in the '80s. You'd pick up the receiver with one hand and spin the dial with the other. Today, dialing is as simple as swiping up and tapping a few buttons—an action eerily similar to what we do to shop online, check emails, read, watch something, and doomscroll.

From the moment I wake up, my day falls into a familiar pattern: reaching for my phone, heading to the bathroom, brushing my teeth, washing my face, making coffee, and diving straight into work at my laptop. When I observe my movements throughout the day, I see how my body takes shape through these actions.

What does my life look like? What do I look like?

When I step back and examine my daily routines, a clear picture begins to emerge—a life shaped by repetition and stillness. My body moves through a familiar loop: sitting, typing, staring at screens, driving from one place to the next. The days are quiet, marked only occasionally by movement—a walk around the neighborhood, a conversation with my son or husband, a commute to the office a couple of times a week, a ping pong match in the evening, or the simple act of sharing a meal.

Most of my time is spent alone, absorbed in solitary tasks. Even when I do connect—with coworkers on a screen or loved ones in passing—the dominant rhythm of my life is stillness: screens, chairs, and the soft hum of modern isolation.

No wonder Edward Hopper's work speaks to me.

As I reflect, I wonder: what shape am I making with my body? Am I even aware of how much time I spend hunched over, slouching, and craning my neck downward? My posture feels unnatural, almost alien to the way humans are meant to move. My spine curls as I stare into

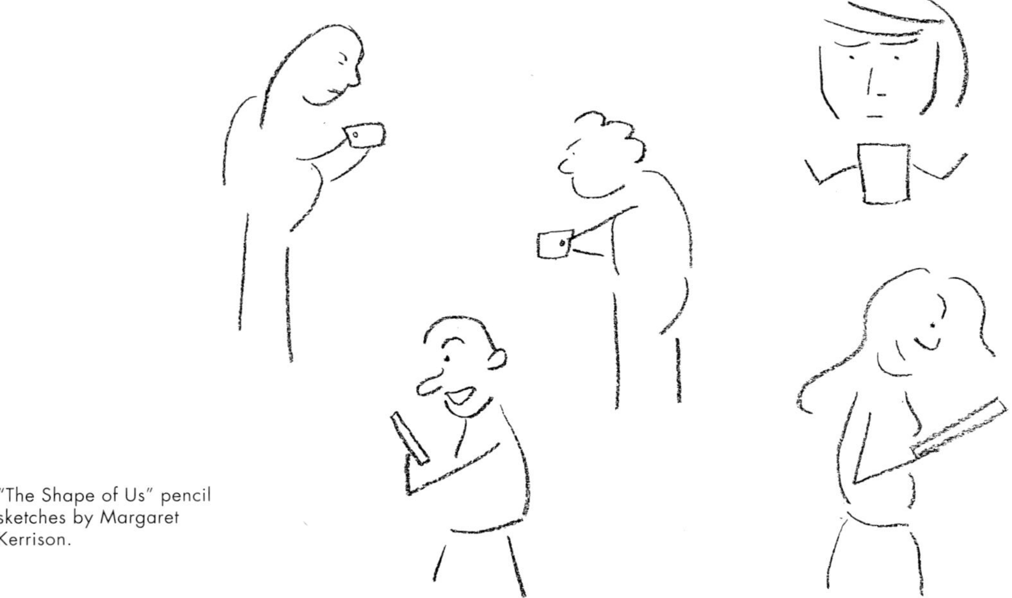

"The Shape of Us" pencil sketches by Margaret Kerrison.

my phone or laptop. My shoulders slump, my muscles tighten, and my gaze is almost always fixed downward. I can feel the weight of these habits on my body, even when I'm not fully conscious of them. None of it feels healthy. None of it feels like how humans are meant to exist.

When I look outside myself, I notice the same patterns everywhere. At the end of the school day, parents stand silently in clusters or sit in their cars, their eyes glued to their phones. Instead of looking up at the sky, the trees, or even each other, they're consumed by small glowing screens. Their bodies are shaped the same way mine is—

hunched, tense, heavy, and solitary. Their expressions are vacant, their postures resigned. It's as though we've all adopted this universal shape of disconnection: shoulders rolled forward, necks bent, eyes lowered.

Where are the actions that remind us we're human? Hugging, smiling, laughing, playing, walking, running, dancing, or even just standing tall and looking up? These actions feel increasingly rare, buried under the weight of our sedentary, screen-dominated lives. I wonder if this is something unique to Los Angeles, a city built around cars, commutes, and individual spaces—or if it's a universal phenomenon spreading across modern society. Are we all becoming isolated, bent into unnatural shapes by the very environments we've created?

And this raises deeper questions: Are we sitting too much? Are we looking down too often, shrinking ourselves into smaller and smaller physical forms? Are we spending too much time alone, separated not just physically but emotionally from those around us? How much of this is a reflection of the spaces we live in—the design of our homes, offices, schools, public spaces, and cities?

Take a moment to think about it: our cities are built for efficiency, not connection. Our homes are designed for comfort, not movement. Our schools and offices prioritize productivity over health. And so, the shapes of our bodies inevitably begin to reflect the shapes of our surroundings. We're molded by the constraints of our environments, whether it's the rigidity of a desk chair, the narrowness of a car seat, or the walls of a room that keep us confined.

And in that reflection, I ask: do we all look the same now? Is there a universal posture, a common shape that modern life has pressed us into? Are we losing the diversity of movement, expression, and connection that once defined us? What would it look like if we were shaped instead by play, joy, curiosity, and connection? If our cities, our homes, and our lives encouraged us to stand taller, move freely, and engage deeply with one another? What shape would we take then? What shape would our lives become?

I imagine those of us with unique skills, talents, and abilities that not only define who we are but also shape how we move through the world. Each person's work brings with it a distinct rhythm, posture, and way of interacting with the environment. Dancers use their entire bodies to move in motion, expressing and creating stories across stages. Construction workers move with purpose, lifting, climbing, and balancing. Artists and musicians engage their bodies in expressive motions, painting on canvases or striking chords with their fingers. Teachers move through classrooms, gesturing with their hands as they guide minds.

These professions require not only mental acuity but also physicality. Each role carry its own rhythm—unique movements that reflect the craft, the labor, and the purpose. These actions shape not just the individual's body but their identity. The way they stand, the way their hands move, even the wear on their clothing tell the story of their work and who they are. I long to see more of a diversity in the shapes we take, a physical connection to the skills we master and the lives we live.

Today, so much of that has changed. Many of us, regardless of our profession, have been evolving into the same shape: sitting, staring at a screen, and typing. Whether you're an accountant, a designer, a writer, or a manager, the work looks remarkably similar on the surface. Our hands hover over keyboards. Our necks crane downward toward glowing screens. Our shoulders round forward, and our backs curve from hours of sitting. Physical diversity in work has been replaced by a uniform stillness, a posture dictated by the tools and technologies we now rely on.

We've outsourced many of the roles that once demanded physical effort. Tasks that required motion—building, fixing, carrying, crafting—are now done by others or, increasingly, by machines. We've designed our lives to prioritize comfort and efficiency, gravitating toward what feels familiar and easy. In doing so, we've avoided the physicality of work, replacing it with a focus on convenience and intellectual engagement.

This shift toward "thinking" jobs over "doing" jobs has consequences. We move less, and the variety of shapes our bodies take throughout the day becomes painfully limited. This lack of movement affects more than just our posture or physical health; it ripples outward into our emotional state and social well-being. Movement is tied to vitality, creativity, and connection. When we stop moving, we risk losing these qualities in our daily lives. We risk losing our humanity and our community.

But what if it were different? What if I consciously reimagined my day—not just the tasks I perform but the shapes my body takes as I move through it? I imagine waking up and starting my day with motion: walking, stretching, or dancing to music. Instead of sitting for hours, I imagine standing, pacing, or working with my hands—building something, creating something tangible. I imagine taking breaks not just to rest but to move, to step outside, to play a game, or to talk with someone face-to-face while walking together. Sharing a meal becomes an act of connection, engaging my hands, my senses, and even my posture as I move around the kitchen. Play becomes part of my day, whether it's chasing my son, practicing yoga, or simply laughing with friends.

The shape my body takes becomes a reflection of the life I want to live. Movement isn't just a chore or a health goal—it's a way to experience joy, creativity, and connection. It's about reclaiming the diversity of motion that makes us feel alive. And just as the shapes of tradespeople once reflected their unique skills and roles, my movements could tell a story of engagement, vitality, and intention.

When I imagine this life, I see more than just a shift in posture—I see a shift in perspective. It's not just about standing instead of sitting or walking instead of driving. It's about allowing the shape of my body to reflect a life that is active, connected, and deeply human. A life that values movement not just for efficiency but for the richness it brings to every moment.

The shape my body takes is informed by the environment and places I inhabit. And the shape I want to take influences where I go to partake in that shape. If I want to walk continuously without stopping, I head to the Lake Hollywood loop or take a short drive to the many beaches along the coast of Southern California to walk without a destination.

I also know that the shape my body makes can influence my surroundings. The way we move, sit, walk, and interact with spaces doesn't just reflect who we are—it also impacts the spaces themselves. Designers, architects, urban planners, and others often pay close

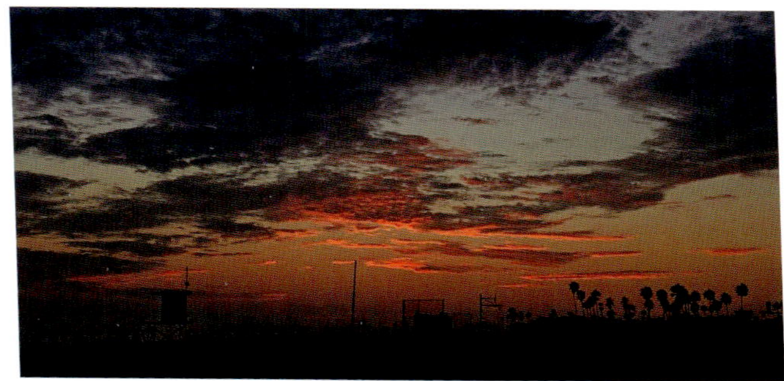

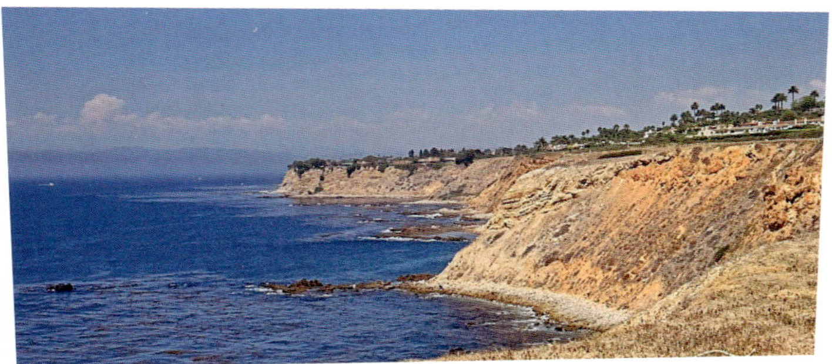

Scenes from Southern
California's coastline.
Photos by Foster Kerrison

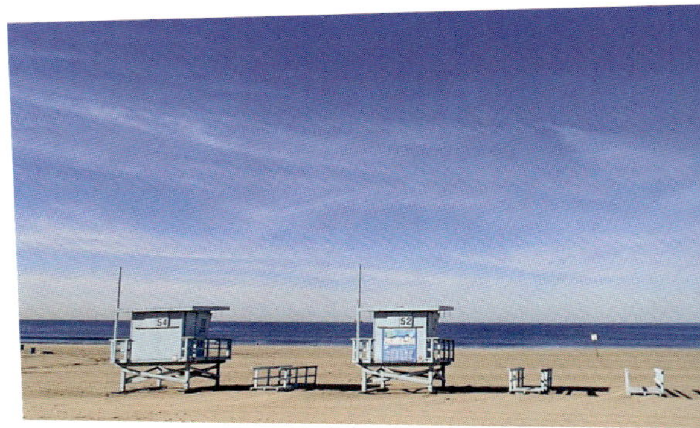

attention to these interactions, studying how we navigate through cities, use public spaces, or inhabit our homes. Their goal, ideally, is to create environments that reduce friction in our movements and bring harmony to our actions. Well-designed spaces can make our routines easier, more enjoyable, and even healthier. For example, a thoughtfully designed park invites us to walk, play, and gather, while a poorly planned one might go unused, leaving us disconnected from the outdoors.

But there's also an unspoken hope embedded in these designs: that someone cares enough to notice how we move, how we gather, and how we live. We hope they consider the ways our environments could encourage more joy, connection, and well-being. What if sidewalks were wider, inviting more spontaneous conversations between neighbors? What if bus stops were designed to have free mini libraries? What if public art represented our diverse cultures? What if workplaces were designed to encourage standing, stretching, or walking, instead of endless sitting? What if public spaces made it easier to connect with others, offering areas for shared activities rather than isolating benches and empty plazas?

We hope that our shapes—our slouched shoulders, our craned necks, our sedentary postures—send a message, sparking a response from those who design the world around us. We hope someone notices the way a comfortable bench can make us linger longer, how natural light in a workspace can uplift our mood, or how tree-lined walkways can bring more people together. When these observations translate into changes, they create environments we're drawn to—places we want to visit again and again because they feel good to inhabit.

In turn, the spaces we frequent begin to influence us. A space designed for movement invites us to move. A space that fosters connection encourages us to connect. Over time, a feedback loop emerges: our actions shape the spaces we use, and those spaces, in turn, shape the people we become. This dynamic interaction—between our bodies and the places we inhabit—has the power to reimagine the way we live, one thoughtful design choice at a time.

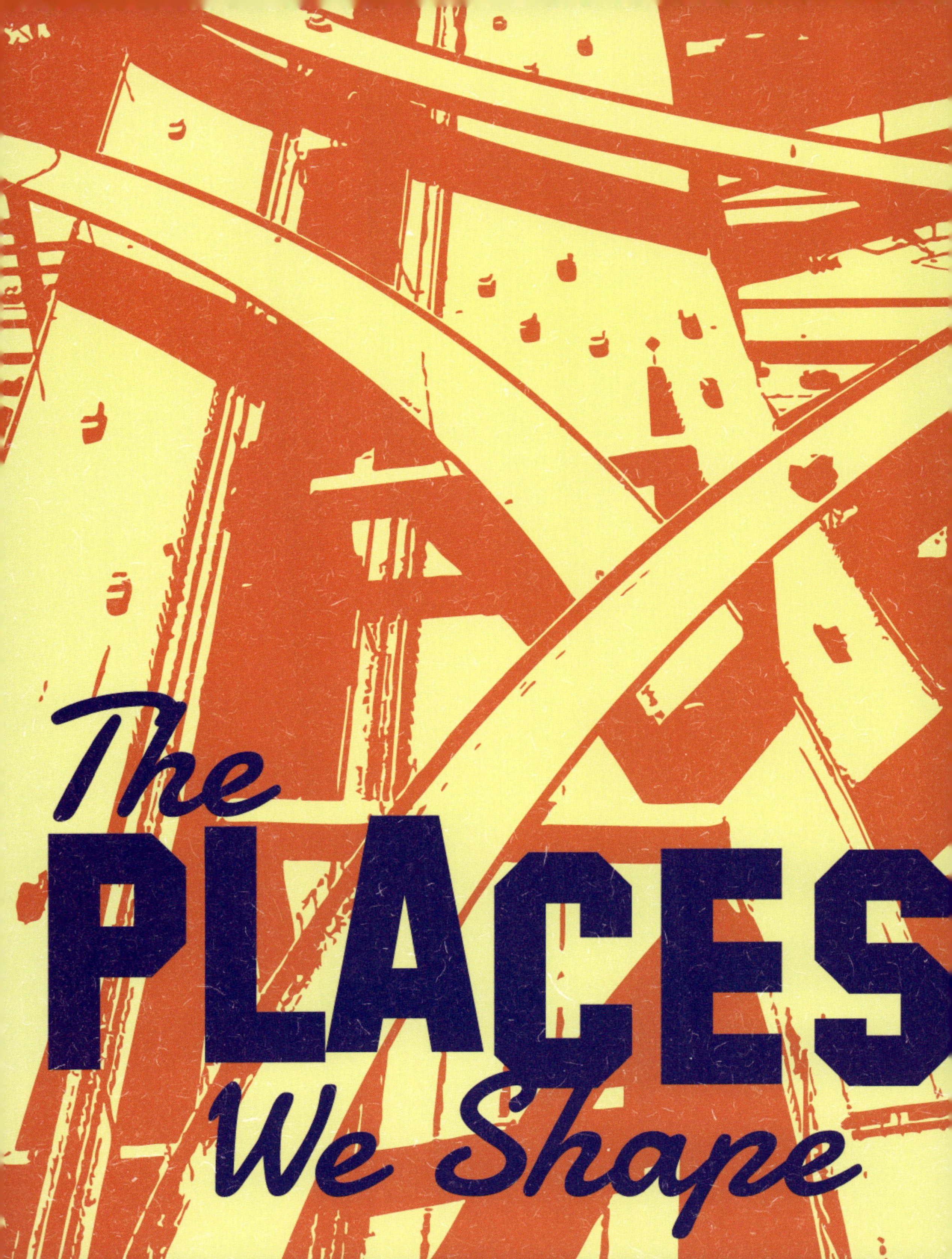
The
PLACES
We Shape

We may assume that a place is passive and inert—that it waits for someone to enter and make it come alive. But the truth is that the places we shape as designers end up deeply affecting all those who enter them and return to them time and time again. While we shape these places, they shape us too. Over time, these spaces alter the way we see the world. They shift our sense of self. And sometimes, without meaning to, they begin telling our stories back to us. We live, work, and play within the spaces we create, and we end up carrying these places within us, no matter where we are.

There are many who carry these places in their art and design. For example, the relationship between person and place is something I feel deeply in the work of Do Ho Suh. His installations of homes, crafted from paper, other mixed media, and sewn from translucent fabric—corridors, staircases, kitchens from previous apartments in Seoul, New York, London—are not reconstructions of physical architecture alone, but of memory landscapes. They are about transition, memory, displacement, and the longing to take one's home with them. Each one is a ghost dwelling, filled with the outline of objects touched a thousand times: a faucet, a doorframe, a buzzer. Walking through them, you feel as though you're inhabiting someone else's life for a moment—but not in a voyeuristic sense. It's deeper. Intimate. As though you're inside someone's memory of a space, the way it exists not in photographs, but in longings.

There's no figure present in Suh's work, and yet the figure is everywhere. The human presence lingers in the decision to recreate a seemingly mundane light switch. In the careful exactness of the radiator pipe. The details of the home capture the figure's focused care, attention, and lingering memory in an effort to preserve something precious and fleeting. The person is the place. And the place becomes a kind of vessel for remembering.

This kind of narrative-through-space resonates far beyond the gallery. I felt a similar intimacy the first time I encountered Liza Lou's *Kitchen,* "a tribute to the unsung labor of women throughout time." At first glance, it's a full-scale domestic installation, a suburban kitchen. But then you realize—it's entirely covered in hand-beaded glass. Every tile, every cereal box, every slice of fruit in a bowl. It's a painstakingly impressive work of art that represents an ordinary, everyday setting. It took Lou five years to make it. And in that devotion, the repetition, the obsession of it all, we come to know the woman who inhabits it. She is not there, but she is everywhere in this dazzling, domestic drudgery. You feel her burden and her pride. Her isolation and her imagination. The space tells the truth of her labor, her longing, her identity—without a single word spoken or a body shown. Sometimes, absence is more powerful than presence.

Another example of a space built not to contain people, but to tell us who they were—even fictional figures—is Michael C. McMillen's *Central Meridian (The Garage)*. It is a dusty, hyperreal "walk-in assemblage" composed of artifacts from the early to mid-twentieth century found in Los Angeles alleys and other sites—a forgotten garage filled with ephemera: a rusty car, oil-stained tools, old bottles, and other curious objects like bodiless doll arms. The garage belongs to no one, and yet it feels like it belongs to someone so particular you can't help but craft their backstory in your mind. This is storytelling not through plot or character arc, but through accumulation of objects. Through things. Through atmosphere. Through imagination. You never meet the person who worked there, but you feel like you know them. You want to understand them. The way they labeled everything, their devotion to particular objects, like their car. You feel their loneliness. It's the architectural equivalent of a diary. The space becomes a form of portraiture.

We often treat physical space as if it's the backdrop to a story. But I've come to see it as a character itself—sometimes the protagonist, sometimes the antagonist, sometimes the silent witness. Especially in the worlds of theme parks, museums, and other location-based experiences, where so much storytelling happens without dialogue. At Disney, for example, the queue is not just a line—it's a stage, a setting for adventure. It sets the mood, reveals backstory, builds emotional scaffolding. It builds fictional history, one object at a time. You never meet the skipper who owns the *Jungle Cruise* outpost, but you know exactly who the skipper is. The desk is a mess. The radio crackles. There are coffee stains on the logbook.

In *Expedition Everest*, long before you encounter the ride's central myth—the Yeti—you walk through a Himalayan village, a base camp turned museum of folklore and missing persons. You examine artifacts, tattered hiking boots, tea kettles, faded photographs, warning signs. The missing climber is never seen, but his presence lingers in every artifact. The person is not the attraction. The space is.

I've felt that same eerie sense of presence-in-absence while walking through the opulent historic mansions of Newport, Rhode Island. At Rosecliff, with its grand ballroom and mirrored halls, or Marble House, with its gold-encrusted panels and imported European furnishings, you never meet the people who lived there—yet you feel them in every detail of excess and ambition. You imagine them standing on balconies, dancing in ballrooms, lounging on chaises. The furniture, the wallpaper, even the wear on the marble steps—each tells a story.

As a designer, I carry all the places I've encountered with me. Every room I've walked through, every set I've created, every environment I've tried to bring to life becomes part of me. They leave impressions on my memory, which in turn shape the spaces I design in the future. They remind me that space is never neutral—that every curve, every texture, every flickering light holds the potential to reveal a character. And that character, in many ways, is a reflection of myself.

And the more I design, the more I realize that the boundaries between self and space are permeable. That my design decisions often reveal more about my past, my preoccupations, my hopes, than I ever intended. Sometimes I catch myself recreating a corridor from childhood. Sometimes a fictional character I'm designing for ends up living in a space I wish I'd had. And other times, I don't recognize what I've made until I walk through it and feel something stir—comfort, nostalgia, curiosity, wonder.

Because, in the end, the places we shape do not remain separate from us. They leave marks. They latch onto us—unbeknownst to ourselves. And sometimes, they reveal who we are before we even know it.

So now, whenever I enter a new place—real or imagined—I ask myself the same questions: Who lived here? What mattered to them? What did they leave behind? What did they carry from place to place?

And perhaps the most important question of all: How will the design of this space shape me and those who come after?

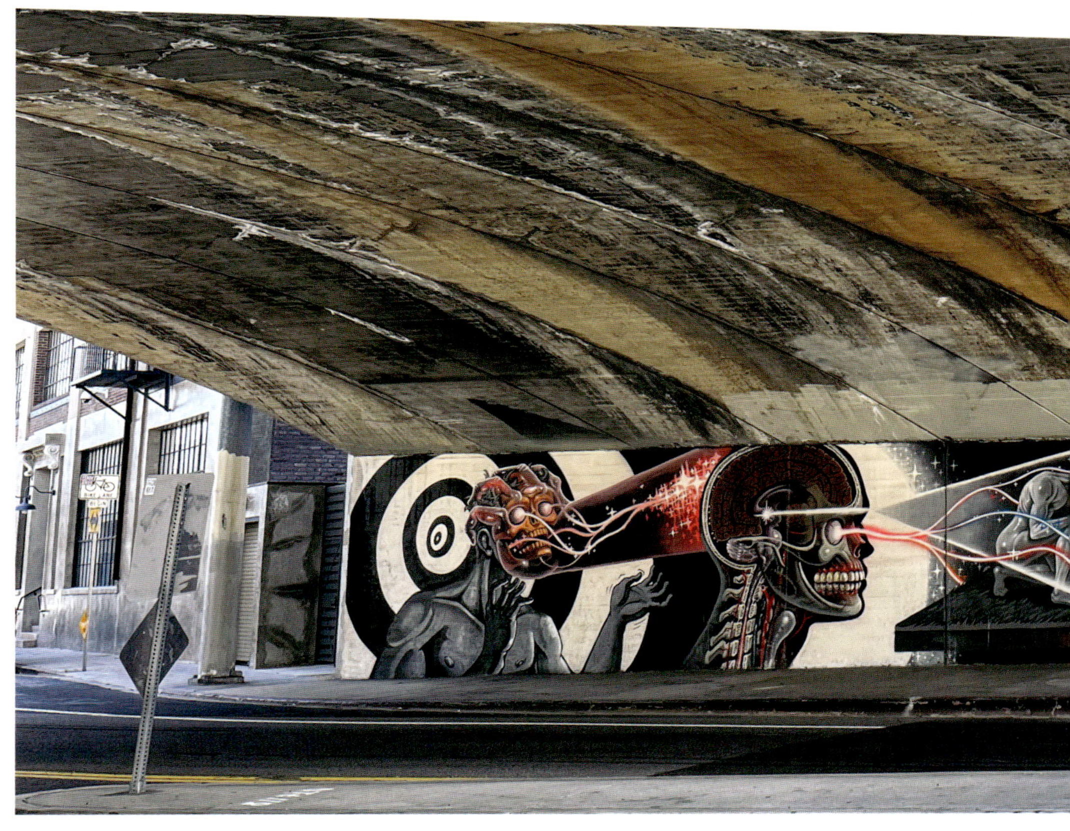

Street graffiti under bridge, Downtown Los Angeles, CA.
Photo by Margaret Kerrison

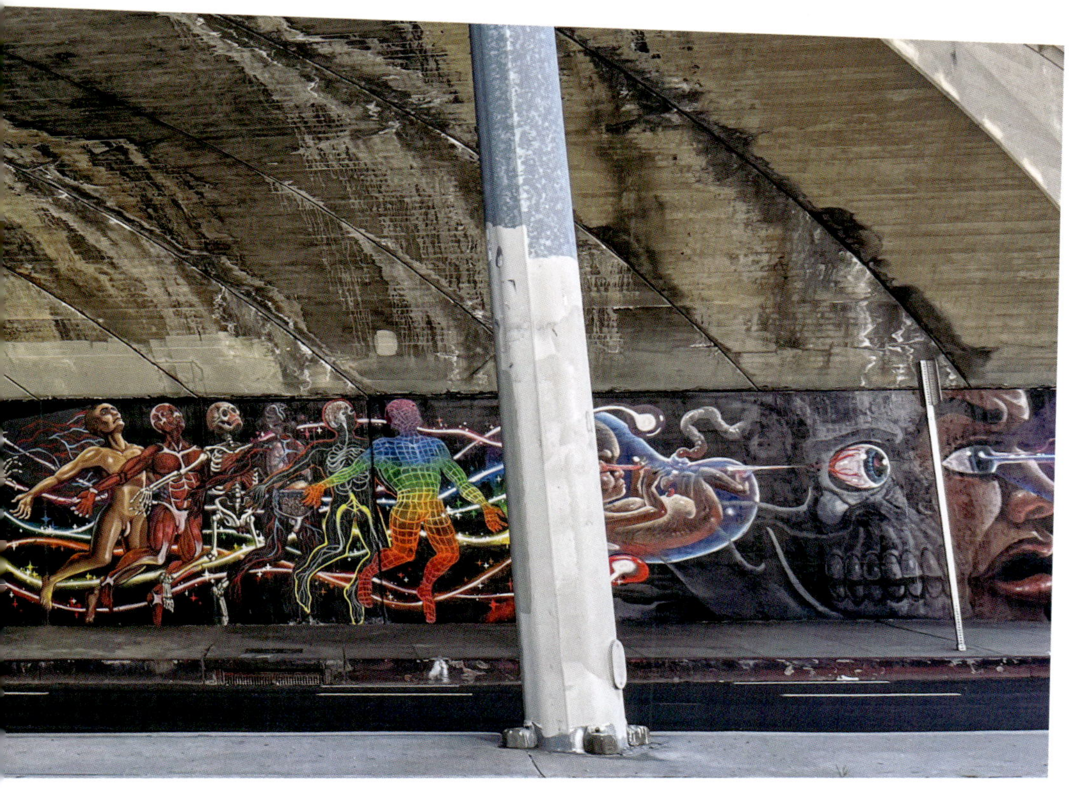

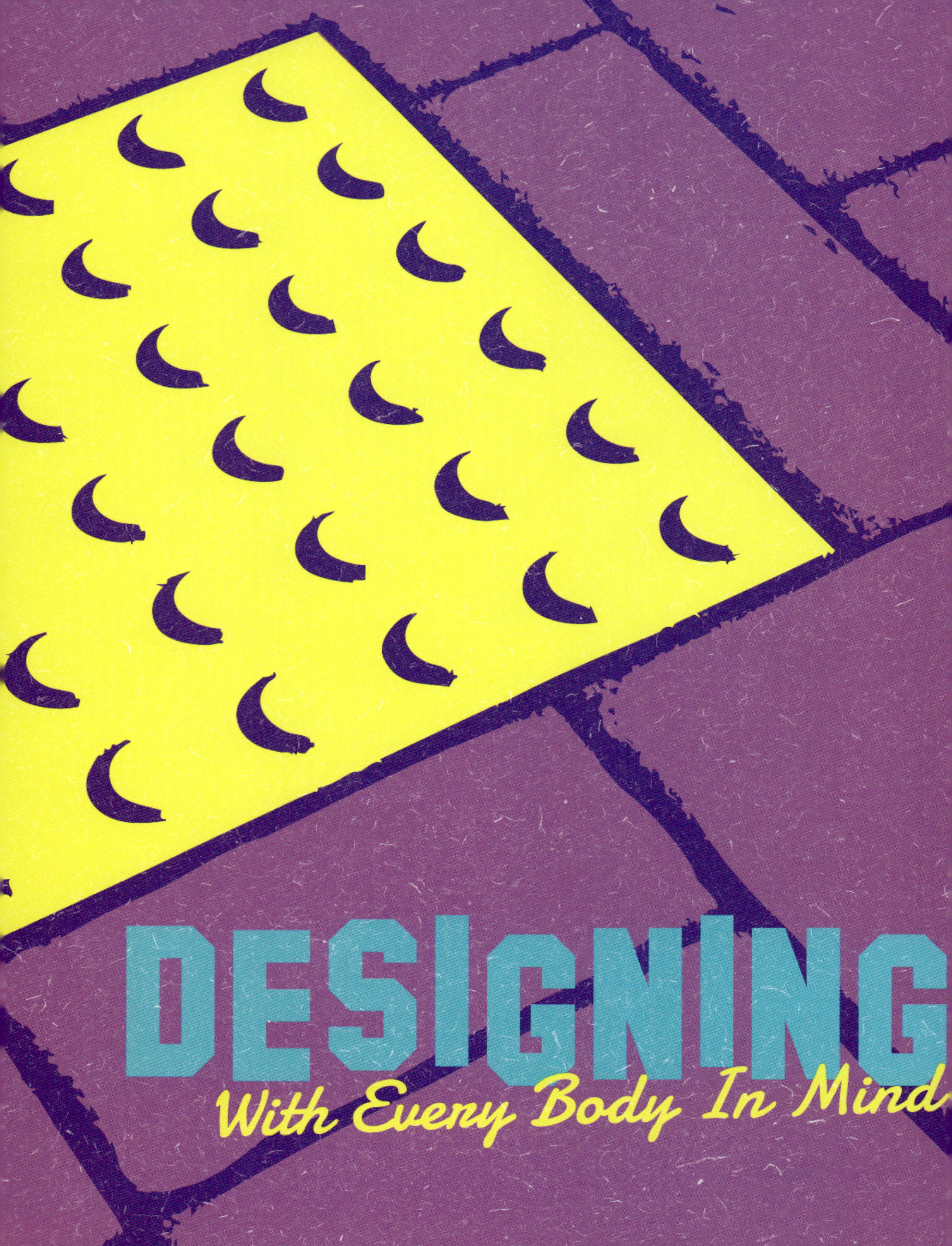
DESIGNING
With Every Body In Mind

When we design spaces, we are not merely shaping structures. We are shaping experiences—worlds in which people live, dream, and remember. And in doing so, we carry a responsibility: to ensure that everyone—regardless of ability, body, or background—can see themselves in the stories we tell and move through the environments we build.

I'm the first to admit that I'm not an expert in designing for accessibility. But I do know what it feels like not to be included, not to belong. To walk into a space and feel—immediately and viscerally—that it wasn't meant for you. That you're somehow on the outside looking in, only a visitor, not a participant. That you can observe, but not partake. I still remember the terrible feeling I had as a small child, unable to go on the thrill rides because I didn't meet the height requirements—how I cried because my siblings could go, but I couldn't. And even today, in experiences where being tall wins, where I can't see the show because I'm short, I never return to those places again, because I feel excluded. It's not a place designed for people like me. I can't experience the place the way it was meant to be experienced.

That feeling stays with you. It lingers in your memory, shaping how you move through the world. And it has shaped how I approach storytelling and design. Because no one should have to carry that weight just to be in a space. Especially not in spaces meant to inspire joy, wonder, and connection.

Too often, accessibility is treated as an afterthought. A compliance checkbox. A ramp added to the side of a building. But true accessibility is not about minimum standards. It's about maximum inclusion. It's about understanding that bodies come in different shapes, sizes, and capabilities, and that our environments should embrace that diversity—not just accommodate it.

As storytellers and designers, we must begin with empathy. That means listening deeply—not only to the loudest voices, but to those often unheard. What does it feel like to navigate a busy plaza with limited vision? To read signage when the words are tiny? To follow a story in a theater when sound is processed differently? These aren't just hypotheticals—they are daily realities for millions of people. And if our goal is to create environments where everyone feels a sense of belonging, those realities must guide our design from the very beginning. Every project should include an accessibility expert—someone who brings the lived experience and perspective of different bodies and abilities into the creative process.

The best experiences aren't just beautiful—they're generous. They invite participation on multiple levels: physical, emotional, sensory. They consider the child in a wheelchair who wants to feel the thrill of a ride, the elderly visitor who needs a place to rest in the shade, the neurodivergent guest who experiences the world through different rhythms and stimuli. As a hypersensitive person, I feel this everywhere I go. I am immediately overwhelmed by loud noises, crowds, and small spaces. My anxiety rises, my heart rate increases, and I feel dizzy and claustrophobic. My first reaction in such spaces is to rush through the experience and leave.

Designing for different abilities doesn't diminish the creative vision—it expands it. It challenges us to be more thoughtful, more innovative. It invites us to build layered stories: ones that unfold through touch, sound, and movement as much as through words and images. It pushes us beyond linear storytelling toward immersive, multisensory worlds where each guest's journey is uniquely their own.

I've learned that some of the most powerful design solutions come not from a place of constraint, but from care. From asking: *What if this world truly welcomed everyone? What if no one ever had to ask for access because it was already built in?* A world where people don't feel "other" but are embraced as one of the many.

We are not designing for the "average" guest. There is no such thing. We are designing for real people—with different needs, different dreams, different bodies. And when we do that well, something magical happens: our spaces don't just function better. They feel better. More human. More alive.

Our environments should reflect the truth that everyone has a place in the story. We design bridges, not gates. Not at the margins, not at the end—but at the heart.

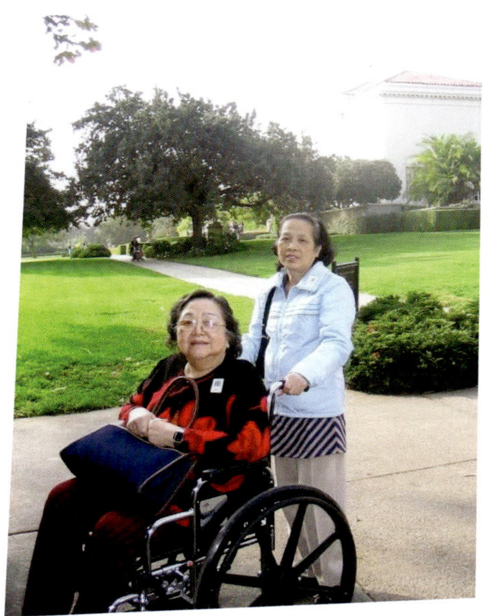

My aunt and I taking turns pushing my *Emak* in a wheelchair around the Huntington in San Marino, CA. Photo by Margaret Kerrison

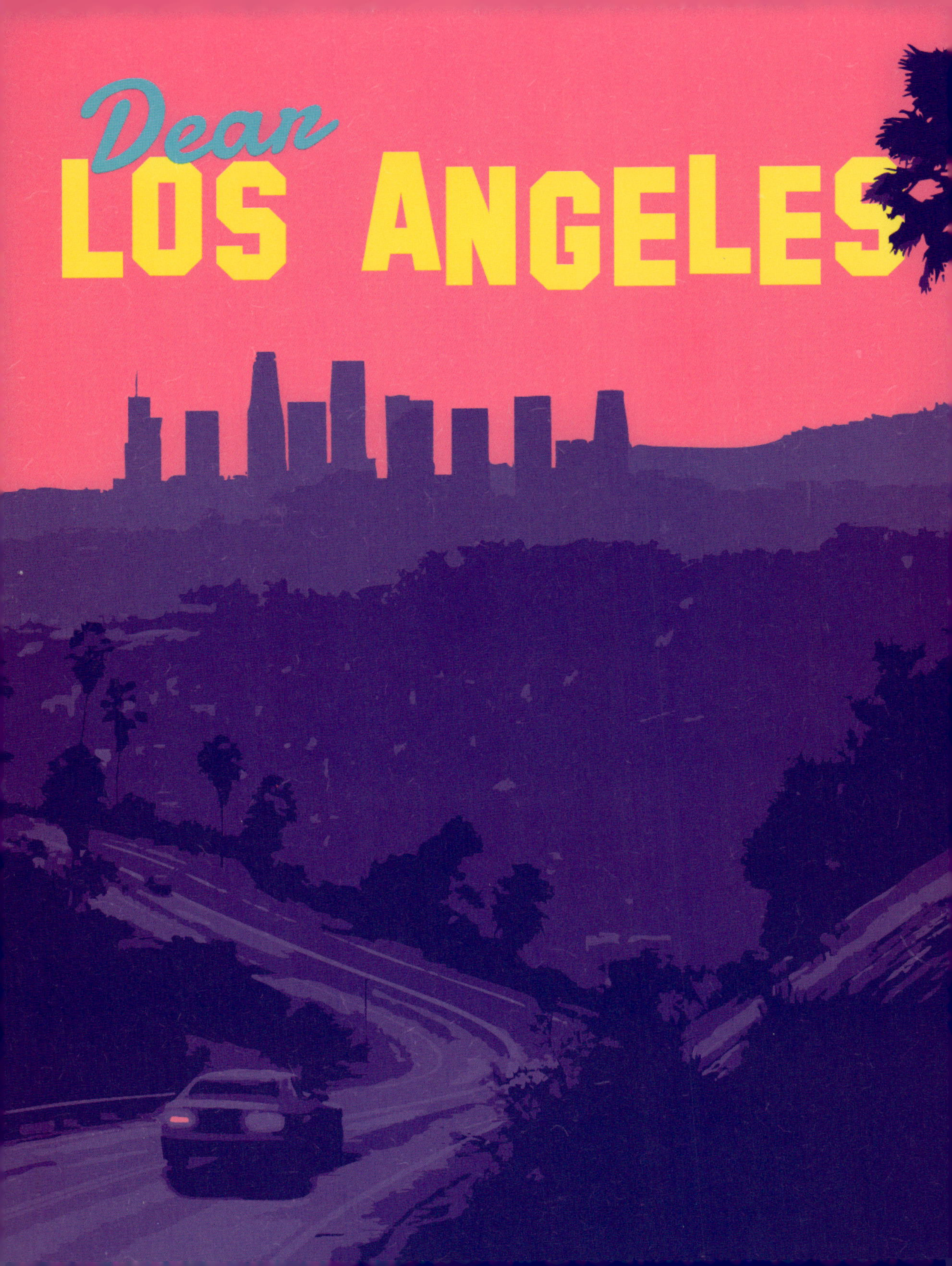
Dear
LOS ANGELES

Dear Los Angeles,

City of scattered dreams and fragmented shapes,
where highways hum like restless rivers,
and mountains stand still,
watching us beneath their quiet gaze.

Your streets are a patchwork of contradictions,
where mansions and tents
share the same checkered horizon.

High art and graffiti collide
on the same streets that carry us
to and fro in our endless busyness.

"How are you?"
"Busy," we collectively reply.

The air carries whispers of ambition,
mixed with smog and salty sea air—
a blend only you could call home.

Your people are islands,
adrift in their cars—
lonely ships on an endless asphalt sea.

Yet, you are more than this.
You are sunsets that spill gold over the Pacific,
families hitting piñatas in Griffith Park,
the laughter of children on the beach
the voices of taco vendors—poets of the curb,
offering their craft with hands that tell stories
of lands far and near.

You are friends sharing brunch
at sidewalk cafés in Los Feliz,
anticipating a visit to the local bookstore,
stealing glances at celebrities
trying to lead normal lives—
as we pretend not to notice.

You are a stage for productivity,
for those who cannot remain still
or focus on any one thing for too long—
a place for dreamers
to act out their soliloquies
in the company of others
who dream similar dreams.

You are the Rose Bowl loop at dawn,
feet striking rhythm against the earth—
the pulse of a city waking up,
stretching into its many lives.

You are the dusty trails of Eaton Canyon,
where strangers nod in quiet solidarity,
children, dogs, friends, and neighbors,
bound by the climb.

But still, I wonder:
what shape do you give us?
Do we bend to your design,
or do we carve our own forms into your ever-changing terrain?
Your grid pulls us apart,
yet your light pulls us together—
a golden thread weaving through our days.

Los Angeles,
you are a mirror and a muse,
a puzzle of dreams scattered across a vast canvas.

Here, anything is possible,
and you dream with us—
always.

A true friend who never gives up on us.
As long as we stay the course,
the road will never end.

But those who can bear it no longer
leave—tired, yet never without regret.

Because they tried,
and that is more than most can say.
We move through you,
and you move through us,
shaping our bodies, our hearts, our stories.

In your chaos, I find reflection.
In your beauty, I find hope.
And in your shadows, I find myself—
searching for the shape I wish to take.

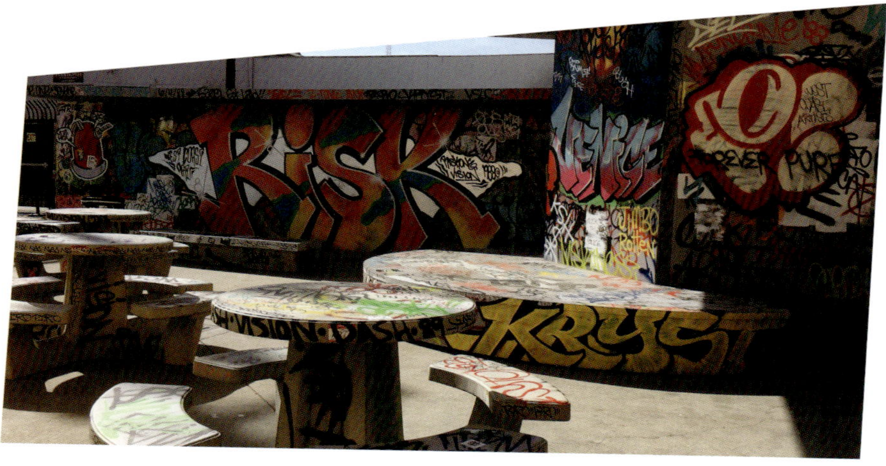

Graffiti art in Downtown Los Angeles.
Photos by Margaret Kerrison

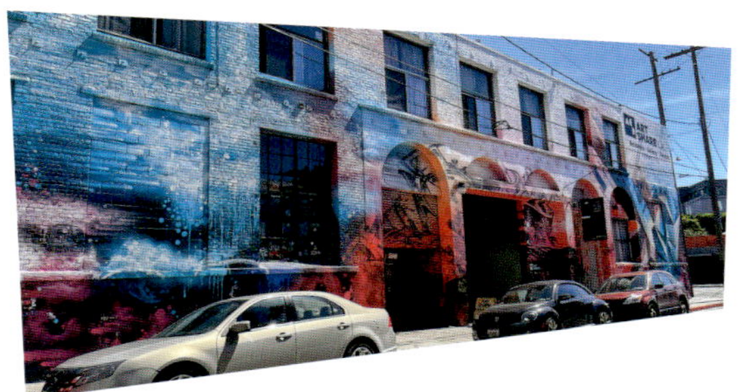

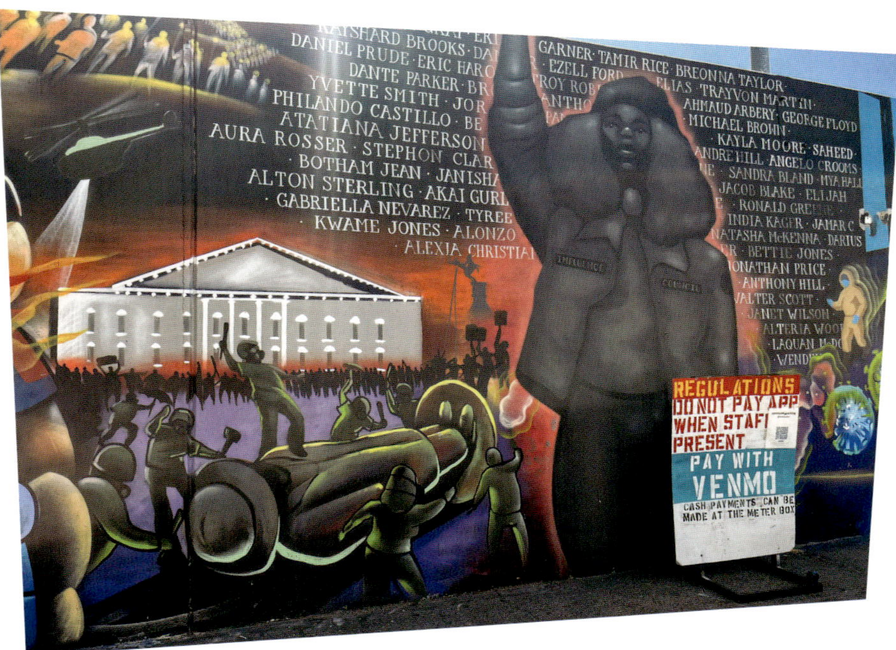
DANIEL PRUDE · ERIC HAR
DANTE PARKER · BR
YVETTE SMITH · JOR
PHILANDO CASTILLO · BE
ATATIANA JEFFERSON
AURA ROSSER · STEPHON CLAR
· BOTHAM JEAN · JANISHA
ALTON STERLING · AKAI GURL
· GABRIELLA NEVAREZ · TYREE
· KWAME JONES · ALONZO
· ALEXIA CHRISTIA
GARNER · TAMIR RICE · BREONNA TAYLOR ·
· EZELL FORD
TROY ROB
ELIAS · TRAYVON MARTIN ·
AHMAUD ARBERY · GEORGE FLOYD
· MICHAEL BROWN ·
· KAYLA MOORE · SAHEED ·
ANDRE HILL · ANGELO CROOMS ·
· SANDRA BLAND · MYA HALL
JACOB BLAKE · ELIJAH
· RONALD GRE
INDIA KAGER · JAMAR C
NATASHA McKENNA · DARIUS
· BETTIE JONES ·
ONATHAN PRICE ·
· ANTHONY HILL ·
ALTER SCOTT ·
JANET WILSON ·
ALTERIA WOO
· LAQUAN M
· WEND
REGULATIONS
DO NOT PAY APP
WHEN STAFF
PRESENT
PAY WITH
VENMO
CASH PAYMENTS CAN BE
MADE AT THE METER BOX

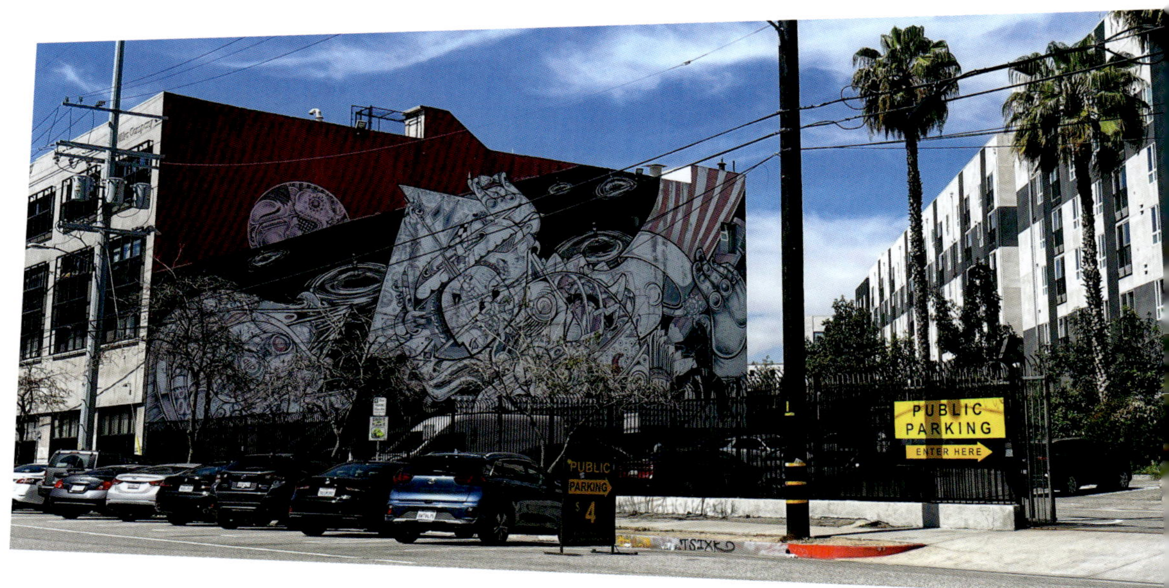
PUBLIC PARKING
ENTER HERE
PUBLIC
PARKING
$ 4

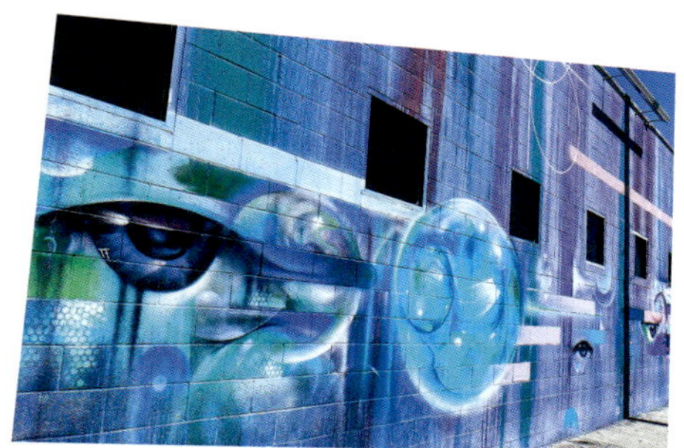

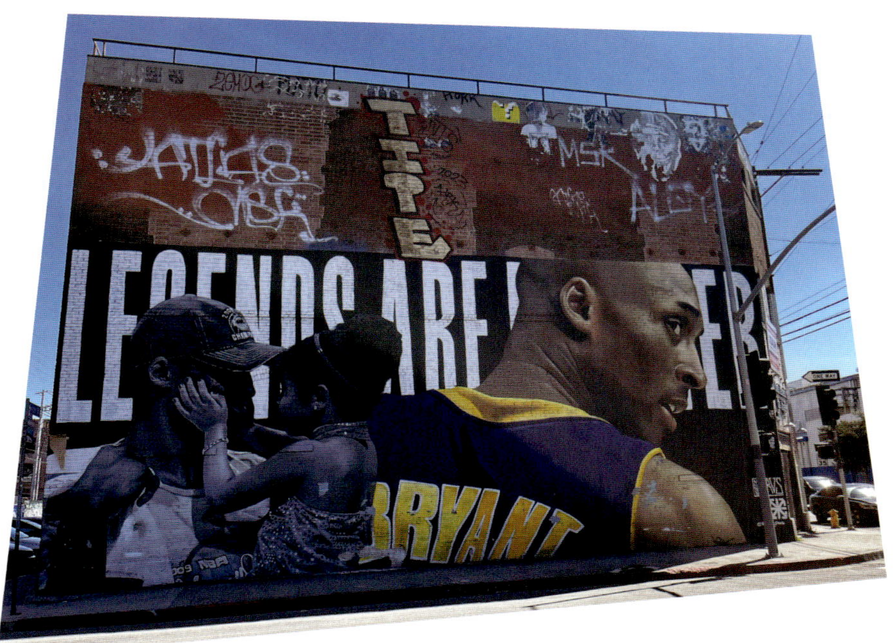
BRYANT

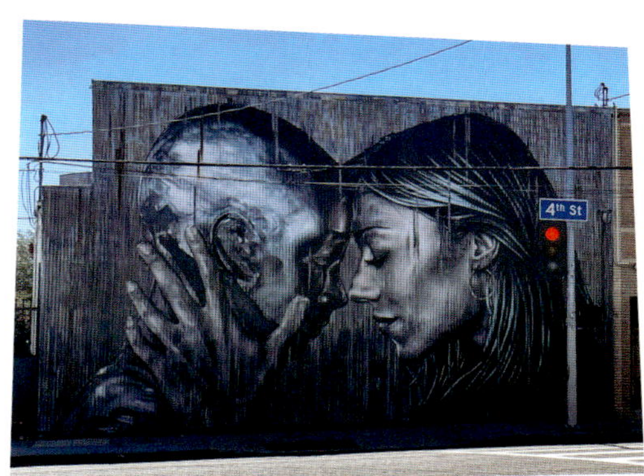
4th St

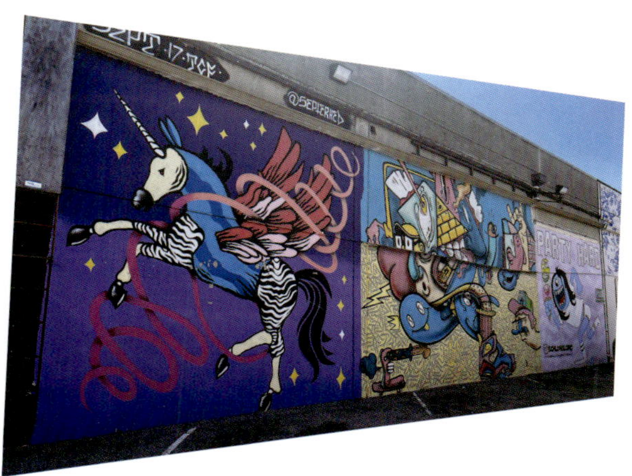

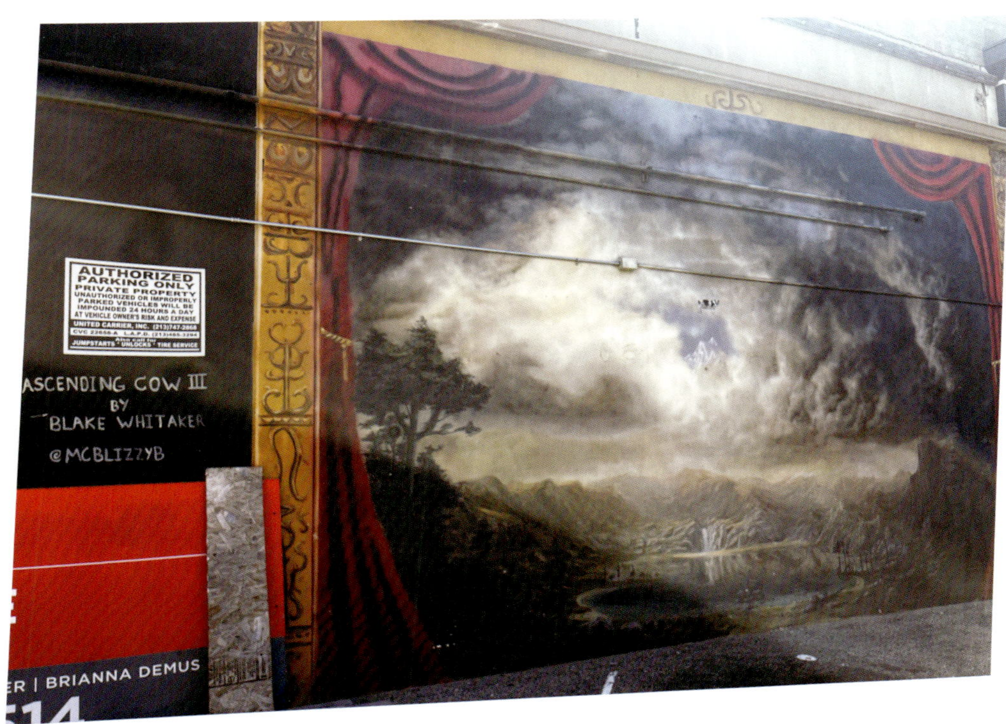
AUTHORIZED PARKING ONLY
PRIVATE PROPERTY
UNAUTHORIZED OR IMPROPERLY PARKED VEHICLES WILL BE IMPOUNDED 24 HOURS A DAY AT VEHICLE OWNER'S RISK AND EXPENSE
ASCENDING COW III
BY
BLAKE WHITAKER
@MCBLIZZYB
BRIANNA DEMUS

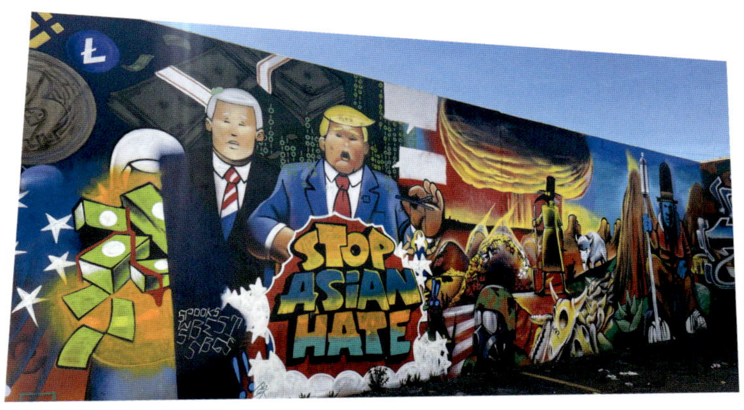
STOP
ASIAN
HATE

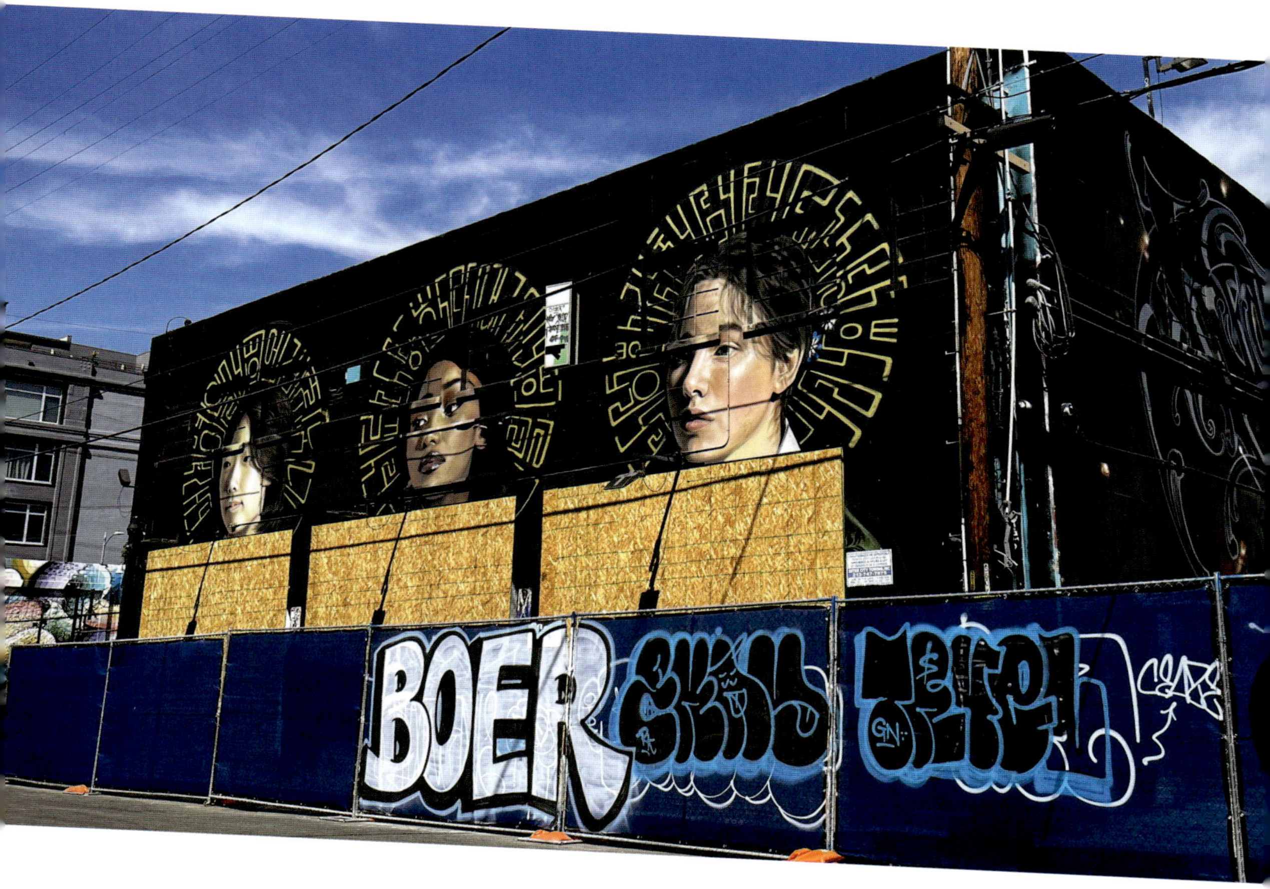

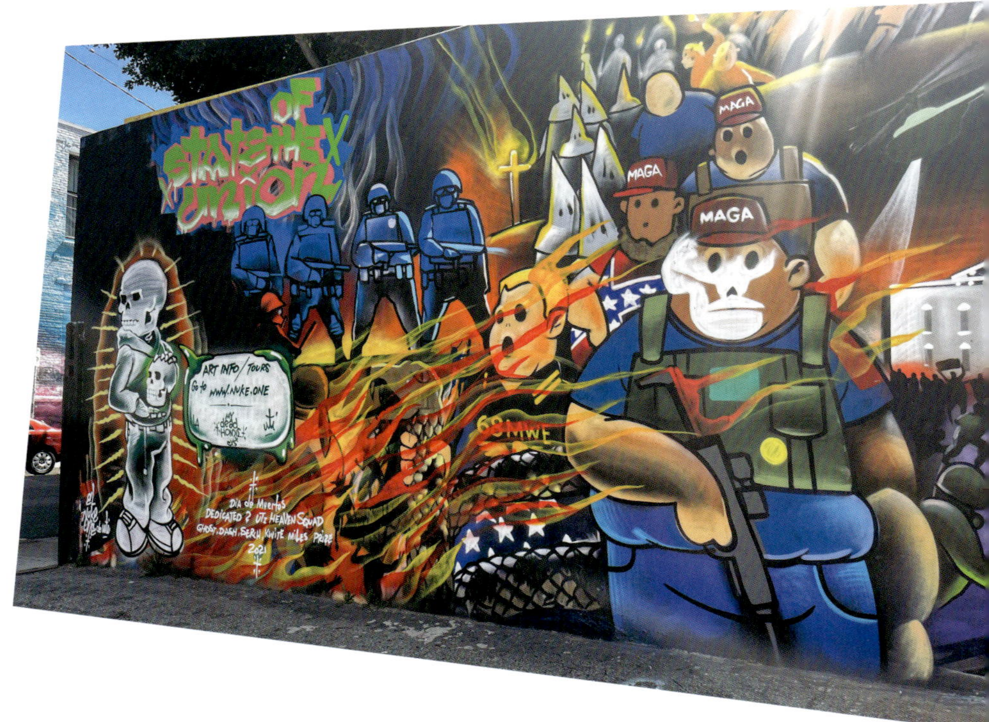

State of the Union
MAGA
MAGA
MAGA
ART INFO / TOURS
Go to www.NUKE.ONE
Dia de Muertos
DEDICATED 2 UTI HEAVEN SQUAD
GHOST, DASH, SERCH, KWITE MILES PRIZE
2021

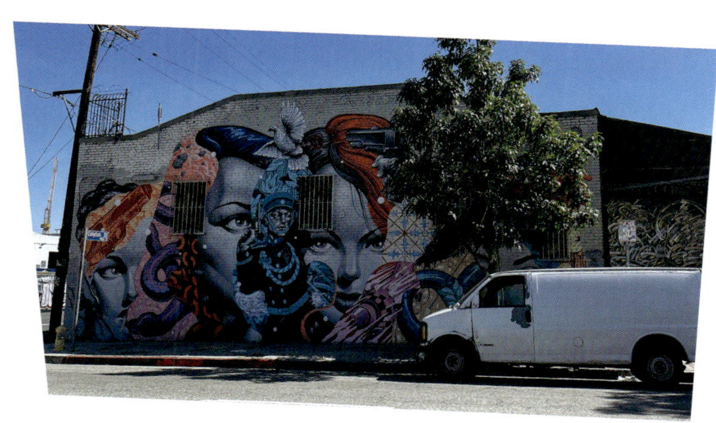

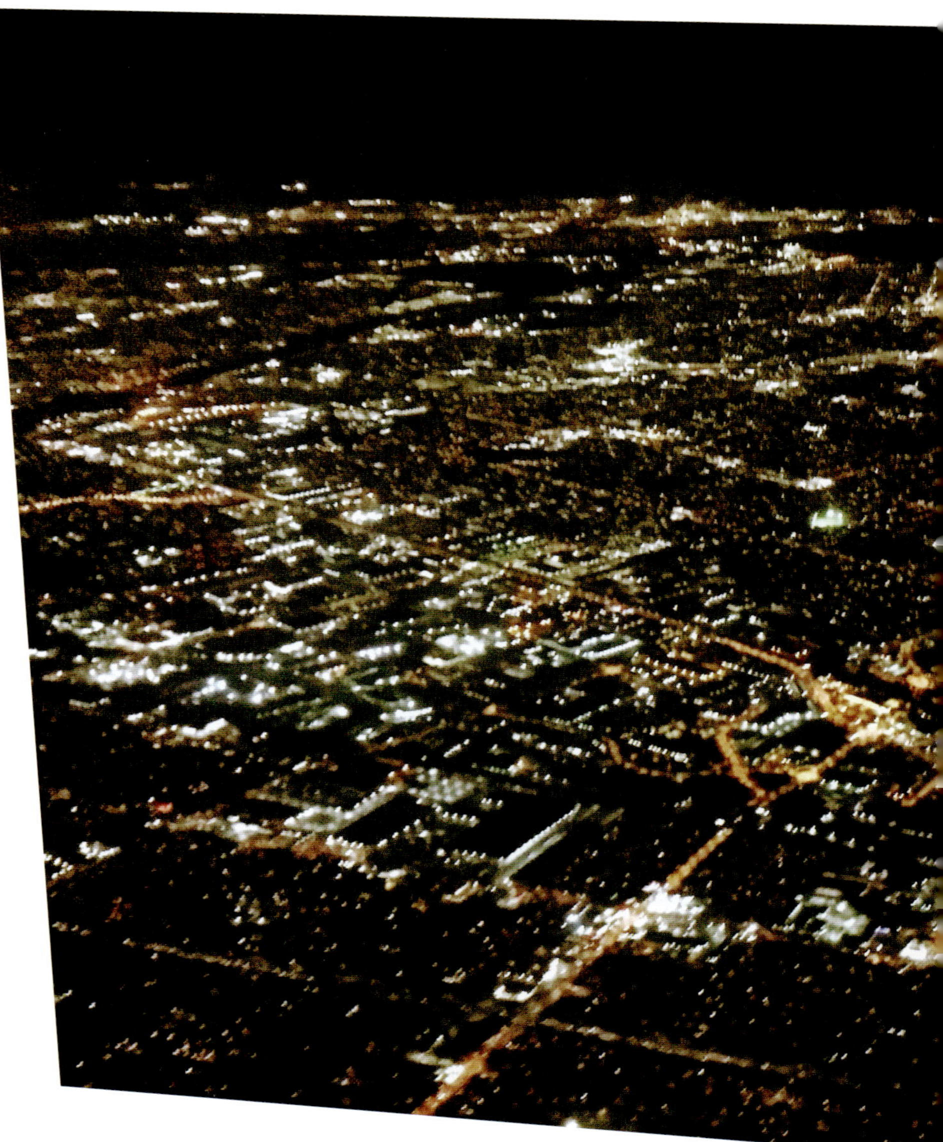

Flying over Los Angeles County.
Photo by Margaret Kerrison

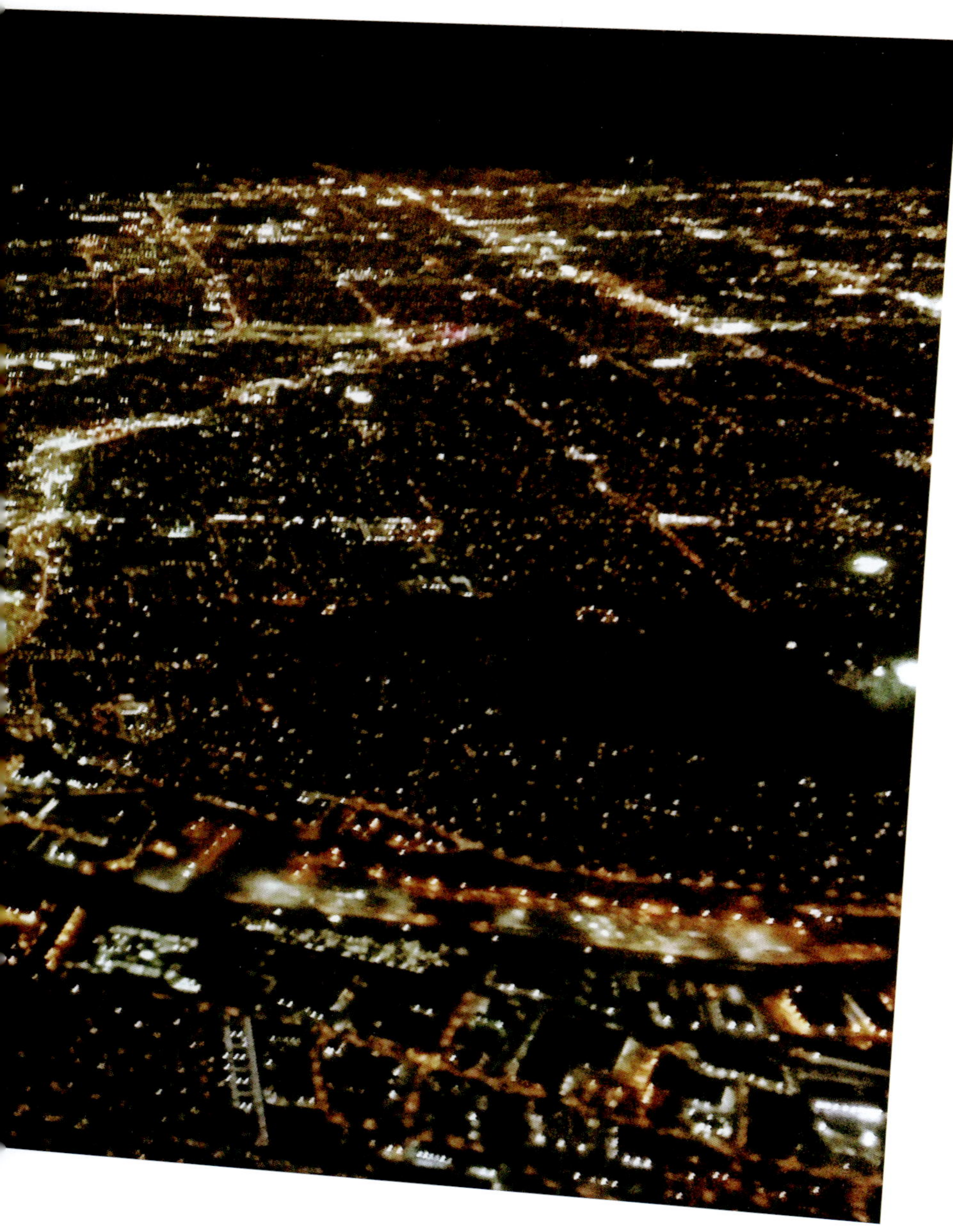

On Being An Introvert In An

EXTROVERTED CITY

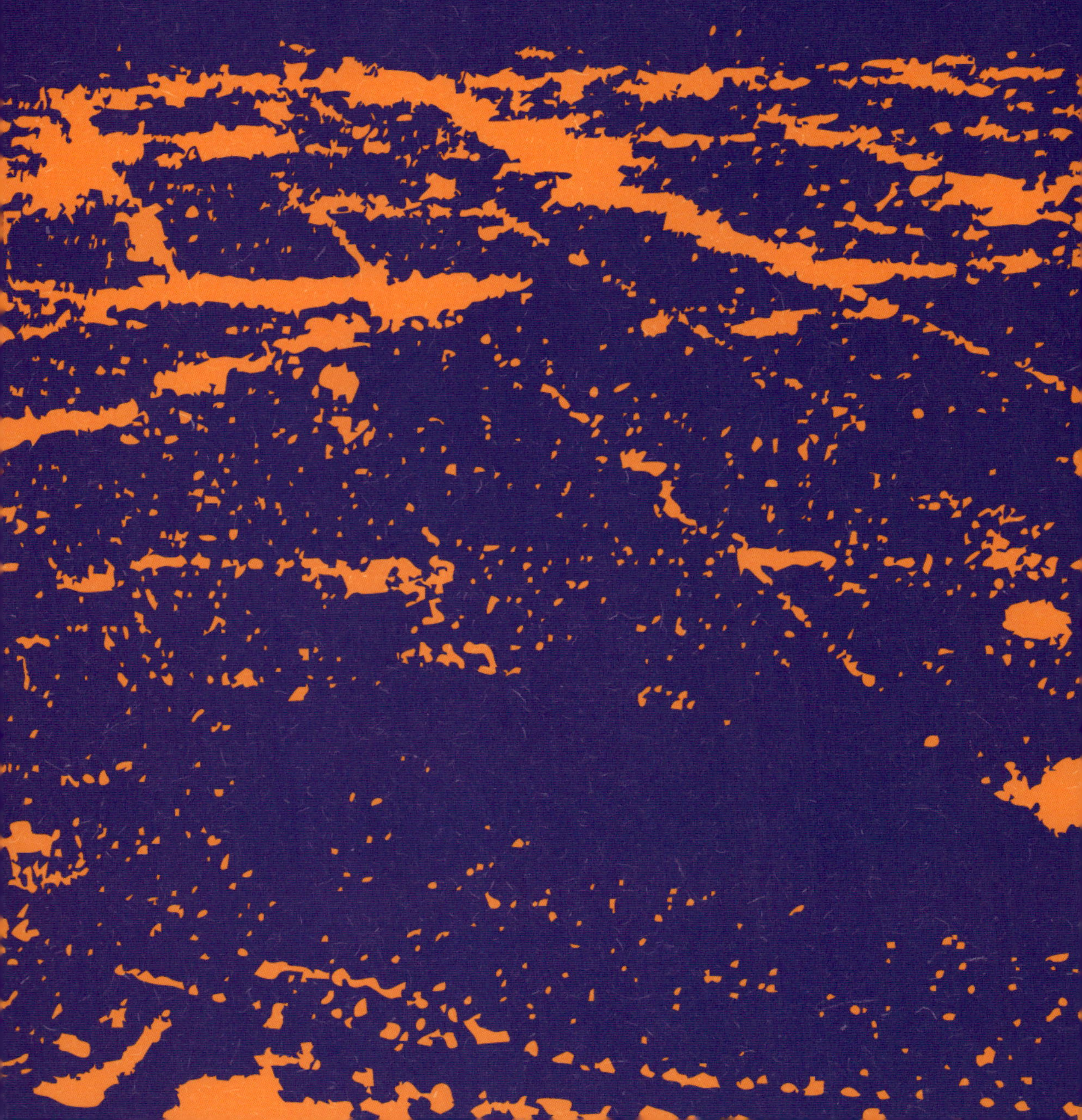

I have always found solace in the quiet spaces of my mind. As an introvert navigating a world that celebrates extroversion, I have often felt like an outsider—watching, absorbing, contemplating—while everything buzzes with endless energy around me. I watch others speak and wonder, should I be this excited too? Should I be this vocal too and share my thoughts as I think them, raw and unfiltered? There is a pressure, an unspoken expectation, to participate in the cacophony of voices that seem to never end.

For me, words require intention. In high school, I was chosen as one of two graduation speakers. The valedictorian was a given; I was the unexpected choice, selected through an audition judged by faculty. I spoke about being someone who listens first—someone who learns by observing, who speaks only when there's something meaningful to contribute. That pattern remains. I move through life quietly collecting moments, listening more than I speak. In many ways, I've become a professional observer.

Los Angeles, with its endless movement and constant reinvention, often feels like a city built for extroverts. But within its sprawling chaos, I've found stillness. Tucked between freeways and palm trees are sanctuaries—bookstores, museums, thrift stores, garden courtyards—where I can hear myself think. In these quiet spaces, I rediscover my voice. Away from the noise, I find clarity, and in that clarity, I find creativity.

Growing up, I mistook my need for solitude as a flaw, something to be corrected. I tried, for a time, to wear the mask of an extrovert, pushing myself into crowded rooms and forcing conversations that drained me more than they fulfilled me. At work, I was celebrated for speaking out and having opinions heard. It drained me to the point that I could no longer function. I left a high-profile job because of it. I thought that success meant being seen, being known, being heard—until I realized that true success for me meant being *understood*, even if only by a few, and honoring my natural inclinations.

It took years to understand that my quiet nature was not a limitation but a gift—a different way of experiencing the world, one that allows for deeper reflection, for storytelling, for weaving immersive worlds that invite others in. I began to understand that my voice had to be intentional and not to fill the void that many immediately want to fill. I started appreciating the strength in stillness, the power of observation, the ability to craft narratives that could transport people without requiring me to be the loudest person in the room.

In Los Angeles, self-promotion is a survival skill. Writers, actors, directors—all must learn to sing their song or risk fading into the background. Like birds in a crowded canopy, they call out for attention: *Look at me! I'm beautiful, smart, talented. I'm exactly what you've been searching for*. It's an ecosystem built on visibility, where silence is often mistaken for absence. But I've come to understand that silence can be a presence all its own—quiet, steady, and powerful. It doesn't need to compete; it only needs to be true.

Introverts are often misunderstood. We are not antisocial; we are selectively social. We are not disengaged; we are deeply attuned. We notice and observe things most people miss. We may not always speak first, but when we do, we speak with intention. And when it comes to creativity, our inner landscapes become fertile ground, rich with the details we collect in moments of silence, in the spaces between words, in the quiet hum of the world around us. Our creativity is cultivated in solitude, nurtured in contemplation, and then carefully shaped before being shared. It is not immediate, nor does it demand instant gratification—it lingers, it simmers, and when it finally emerges, it is fully formed, intentional, and impactful.

For those who, like me, find inspiration in solitude, the challenge is not in generating ideas but in balancing the need for retreat with the necessity of engaging with the world. Creativity does not exist in a vacuum. Stories are meant to be shared, art is meant to be seen, and experiences—no matter how deeply personal—are ultimately enriched by human connection. The key is in finding equilibrium: honoring the need for solitude while embracing the moments of interaction that nourish and expand our perspectives. The city can feel overwhelming, its energy unrelenting, but I have learned to let it inspire rather than consume me. I absorb its stories, its textures, its contradictions, and then retreat into my sanctuary of thought to transform them into something new, something meaningful.

Narrative placemaking has become an essential bridge between my introversion and the external world. Spaces hold stories, and through careful curation, they can become immersive experiences that welcome others into our inner landscapes. I find comfort in designing places that evoke emotion, memory, and meaning—environments that speak in hushed tones rather than demanding attention.

Whether through storytelling, themed spaces, or interactive design, placemaking allows me to share my world without the exhausting weight of constant social engagement. It transforms solitude into a gift I can offer others, inviting them into a narrative crafted with intention and depth. It is an extension of my mind, an external manifestation of the world I cultivate in my quiet hours, a way of connecting without draining my energy. Through these spaces, I can speak without speaking, tell stories without uttering a word, and invite others to experience the world as I see it—layered, intricate, full of quiet magic.

In Los Angeles, I have learned to navigate this balance by creating intentional boundaries. I schedule time for solitude just as I would an important meeting. I seek out places that offer respite from the city's energy—quiet bookstores, hidden gardens, the rare, empty stretch of beach. I choose meaningful interactions over obligatory ones, allowing my connections to be deep rather than wide. And most importantly, I have learned to trust that my introversion is not something to overcome but something to embrace, to nurture, to celebrate. It is the wellspring of my creativity, the source of my clarity, the essence of who I am.

If you, too, find yourself feeling overwhelmed by a world that never seems to pause, know that your quiet nature holds power. Your creativity is not hindered by introversion; it is shaped by it. Let your inner world be a source of strength, a wellspring of ideas, a sanctuary in which your voice—quiet but resonant—can emerge, ready to be heard. Embrace your stillness, lean into your truth, and know that the stories you carry within you are waiting for the right moment, the right space, the right way to be shared.

Beach scene, Santa, Monica, CA.
Photo by Margaret Kerrison

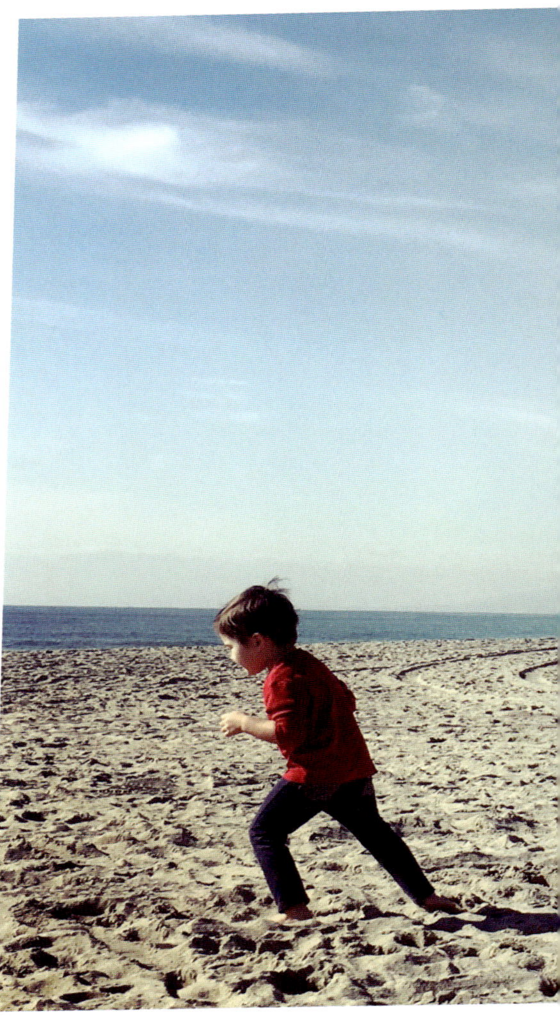

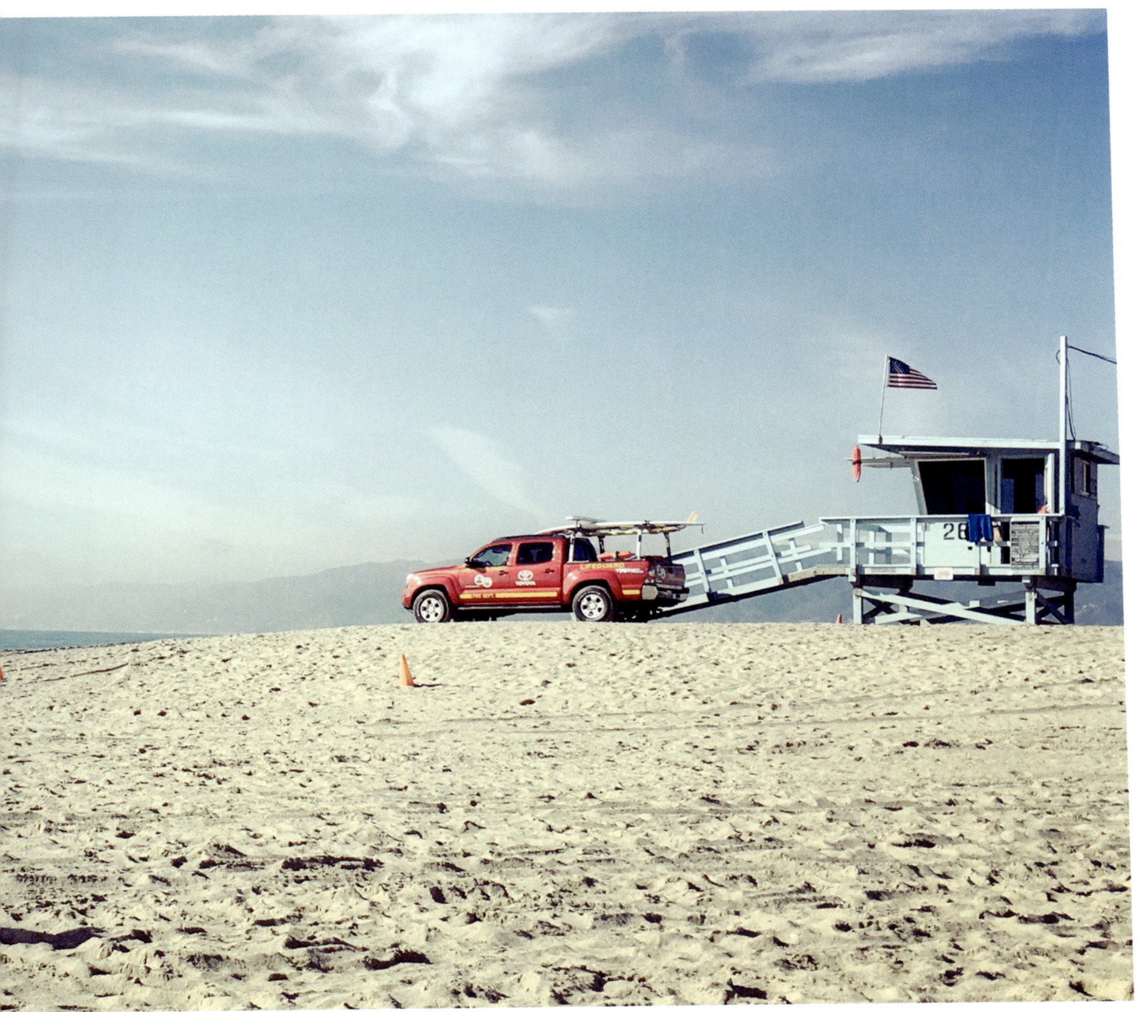

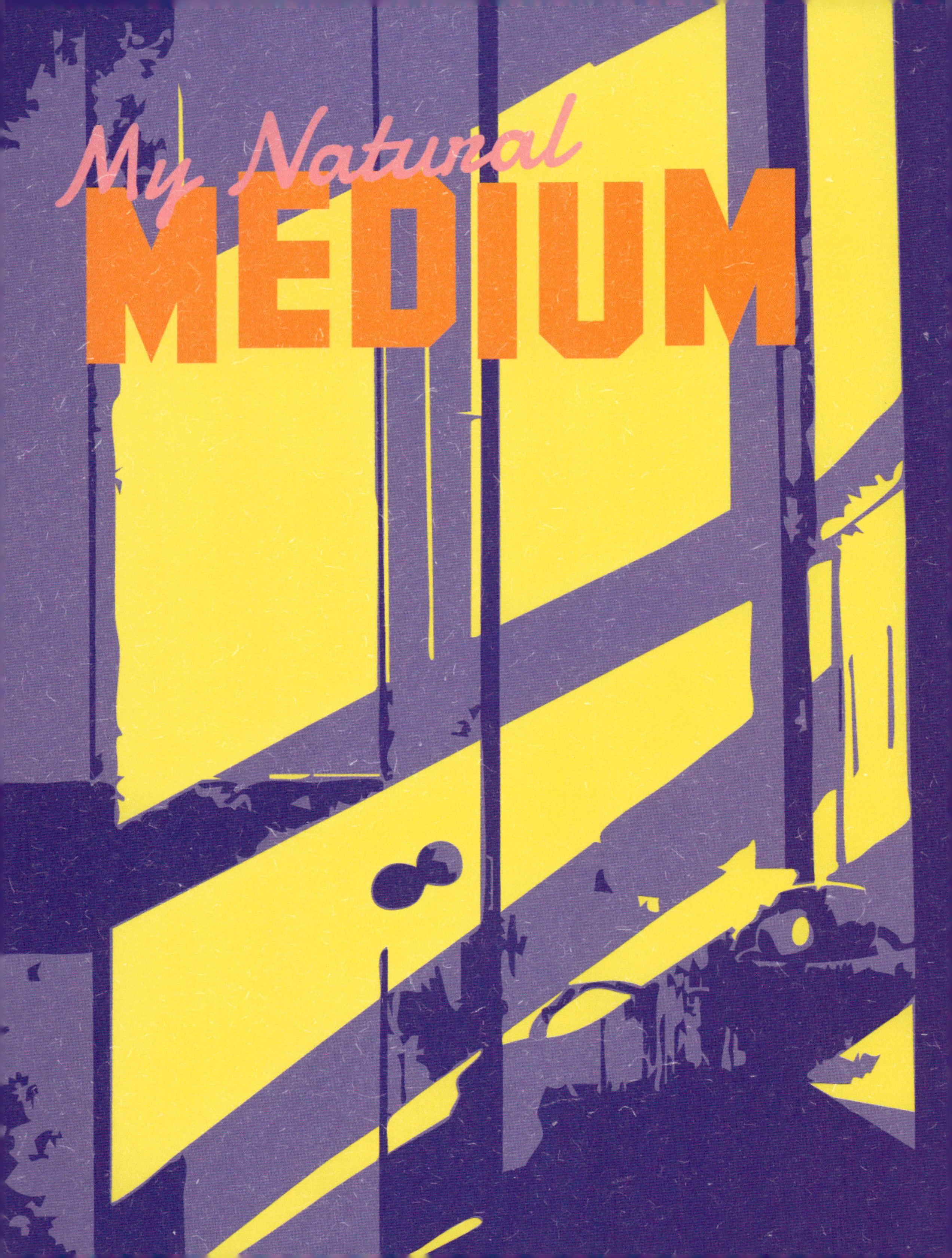

My Natural
MEDIUM

I was recently invited to speak on a recorded podcast session for the annual conference of the Arts, Media, and Entertainment Institute—a nonprofit organization that equips educators with the tools and training they need to empower the next generation of creative workers. In essence, it was a space for teachers to be inspired about how they can better teach their students.

During my conversation with the moderator, she was struck by the way I described writing as my "natural medium." I explained that writing is what comes most naturally to me, and that each of us should recognize and embrace our own natural medium. If you're naturally drawn to making visual art, why force yourself into another form? If you're a natural performer, why not lean into acting or storytelling? Someone else's natural medium doesn't have to be yours. The key is to find your own—and once you do, things begin to fall into place. Your path starts to make more sense, and your creative pursuits feel more aligned with who you are.

I've met so many people who say they want to write a book someday. But when I ask why they haven't started, the answer is usually, "I don't have the time or energy." My honest response is: if writing is truly your natural medium, you will make time. You will give it your energy. And if you don't enjoy writing, don't write. Maybe you're a talker—start a podcast or a YouTube channel. The finished product that inspires you likely came from someone who embraced the process. You have to love the process in order to create the product. You have to commit to the grind—the messy middle. That's the only way anything meaningful gets done: when you love the doing, not just the outcome.

I wake up around 4 a.m. every day to write for myself. This book came out of those early hours—two to three hours of quiet focus every morning. Writing is my natural medium. I do it whether or not I get paid for it. I write in the morning, and I journal at night. It's just who I am.

Know thyself. Know your natural medium.

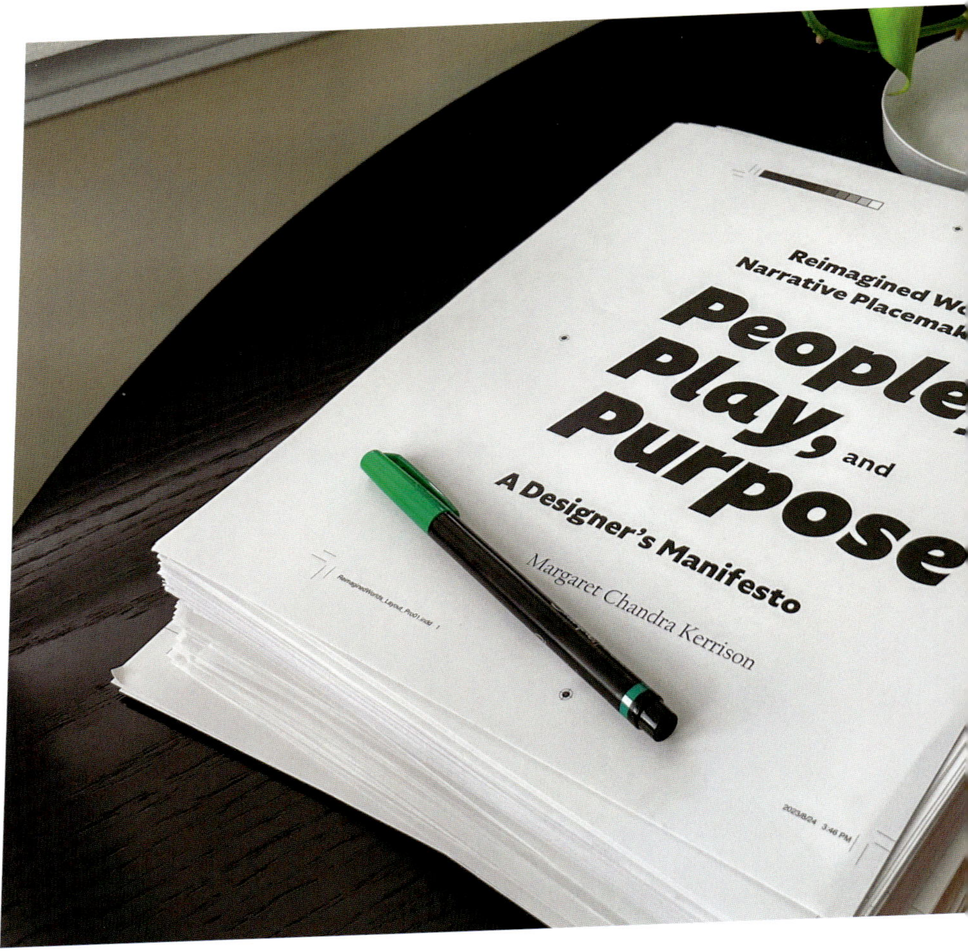
Play,
Purpose
and
A Designer's Manifesto
Margaret Chandra Kerrison

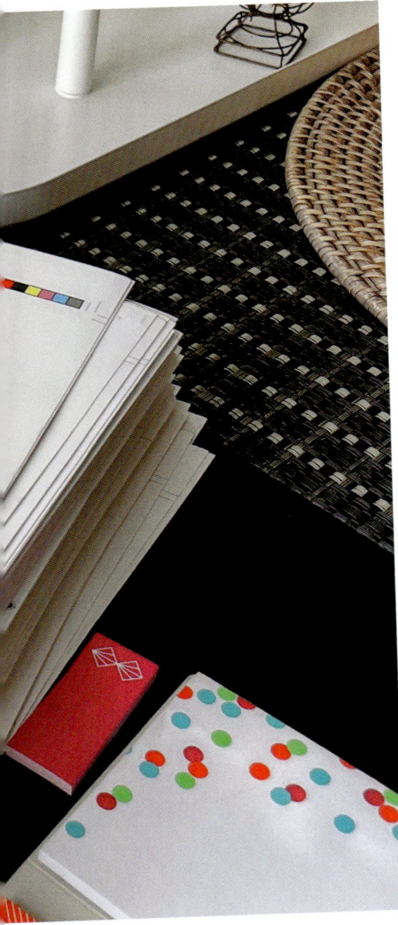

Embracing my natural medium, writing and editing my book *Reimagined Worlds: Narrative Placemaking for People, Play, and Purpose* (ORO Editions, 2024). Photo by Margaret Kerrison

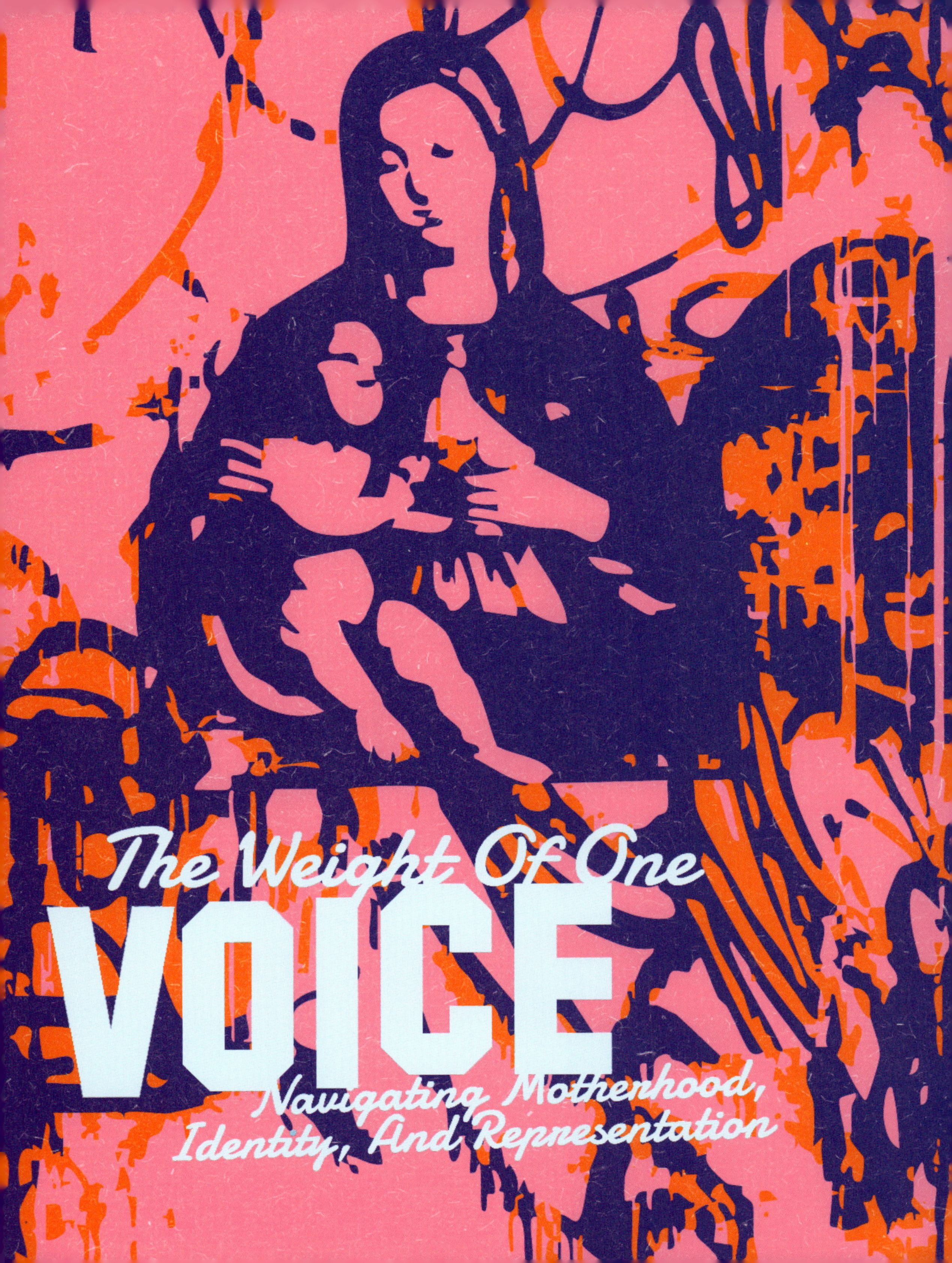
The Weight Of One
VOICE
Navigating Motherhood,
Identity, And Representation

There's always a moment when I walk into a room and realize I'm the only one like me. The only woman. The only mother. The only immigrant. The only person of color. The only one who has lived across countries and cultures, crossing oceans and expectations to stand in that space. The only voice carrying the weight of multiple identities.

That moment has visited me many times throughout my career. And each time, I've had to make a choice: shrink or show up fully.

I chose to show up. Not once, not twice, but again and again.

But showing up has never been simple. In those moments, I don't just arrive as Margaret, the storyteller—I arrive as a stand-in for many, proof that people like me can belong here.

The responsibility is heavy, unspoken, and relentless. Staying silent might have felt safer at the time. But I've learned—sometimes painfully—that silence also means invisibility, not just for me, but for everyone I represent.

And that feeling of safety? It's short-lived. Because every action we take—or choose not to take—ripples through the course of our lives.

We are what we do—defined more by our actions than our intentions.

As an introvert, it took time—and courage—to speak up. To be present with intention. To share an unpopular opinion or ask an uncomfortable question, knowing it might not land easily. But I took that chance, every time.

I questioned cultural appropriation. I asked why the female character was always sidelined or stereotyped. I challenged tokenism. I wondered why the hero always had to be a man.

And for that, I was often met with resistance.

"Why change it if it works?" they ask.
"No one will believe that." they said.
"The audience won't like that."
"No one will notice."
"Why does it matter?"

But it *does* matter. Every choice we make as designers carries weight—because every choice is felt.

I wasn't taught to speak this way. As the youngest child—and a girl—in a Chinese-Indonesian family, I learned that girls and women were meant to be seen, not heard: to listen more than they spoke, and to survive by staying pretty, being patient, and keeping small. But I was lucky. I went to an American school where I learned to embrace my voice. I had teachers who encouraged me to show up and speak up at every chance I got. I also had my grandmother—a fierce, formidable woman who ran a hospital in Surabaya, Indonesia—who modeled something different. She was assertive, generous, and unapologetically loud. She built up other women. She put them in positions of power. She was the one who told me, before I moved to the US, "Don't take everything from Americans. But take their courage. Be brave."

So I tried. And bravery became my compass. I functioned with an attitude of fearlessness; of being true to myself with nothing to lose.

In the creative industry—especially one still dominated by the same voices—quietness often leads to invisibility. Overlooked ideas. Lost opportunities. Stories that never get told. The kinds of stories that could shift culture, they never even enter the room.

So I started speaking—carefully at first, then more boldly. I asked the questions others avoided:

What stories aren't we telling?
Who's missing from this world we're building?
How might this experience feel to someone outside this cultural context?

They weren't always easy questions, but they were necessary. They came from a place of care—for the craft, for the audience, for the future.

Becoming a mother added a new dimension to my journey. My son—multiracial and multicultural—gave me a renewed sense of time, purpose, and legacy. His presence in my life sharpened my focus. Every project I touch now carries the echo of, *Would I want my son to experience this? Would he feel seen in the world we're creating? How would he feel when he walked away from this experience? Will he feel like he's stepping into a better, more hopeful world?*

These questions ground me. They drive me to keep going, even when I'm exhausted. They add to the emotional weight of this work—navigating creative challenges while shouldering invisible labor, all while proving that motherhood isn't a barrier. It's an amplifier of purpose.

Still, the hardest part isn't always the work. It's the isolation. Because when I enter a room, people don't just see me—they see every role I represent. I don't get to be *just* a creative, a luxury many of my counterparts enjoy. Every word I say can feel like it speaks on behalf of all women, all immigrants, all mothers, all people of color. The pressure to be right—to avoid a misstep—is constant. People like me are held to a different standard. We can't make too many mistakes, because people will notice every single one. I imagine, in their minds, they say, *"I knew it. She doesn't have what it takes."*

But it's not imposter syndrome I'm feeling—it's frustration. Frustration from watching the same patterns play out again and again.

And it's not just in my head. I see the consequences. Women like me are passed over for promotion, fired, or the first to be laid off.

But that pressure has taught me something profound:
My voice matters.

Silence might feel easier, but it won't move us forward. Truth-telling—especially when rooted in identity, lived experience, and compassion—is our most powerful tool. It's how we begin to shape an industry that reflects the real world, not just a narrow slice of it.

I don't claim to speak for every woman, every immigrant, every mother. But I do speak as one. And I speak with the hope that one day, I won't be the only one in the room. That no single voice will have to carry the weight of so many others.

Until then, I'll keep showing up. I'll keep using my voice, even when I'm tired. I'll keep questioning, challenging, encouraging—and imagining a future where inclusion isn't a trend, but the very foundation of our industry.

Because themed entertainment isn't just about rides or shows. It's about stories. And stories are nothing without truth.

I've learned that being a minority is not a deficit. It's a gift. It means I carry with me a perspective shaped by complexity, empathy, and a lifetime of navigating between languages, values, and cultural codes. My multicultural background allows me to see what others might miss—and to build experiences that speak across boundaries.

I don't just tell stories.
I build connections.

Yes, I've had to speak louder in rooms where I was underestimated. I've had to advocate not just for myself, but for storytellers and audiences who have yet to be seen or heard. I've had to navigate a system not built for women who pump breastmilk between meetings or leave early for school pickup—or who don't fit the myth of the "creative genius."

But I've also seen change.

Many of my strongest champions are men. I've seen diverse teams build richer, more resonant experiences. I've seen younger creatives find strength in their voices, power in their differences, and courage in their vulnerability.

I've had the privilege of mentoring others and showing them that you can be both a mother and a maker—that you don't have to choose.

The future of this industry—and the future of the worlds we create—depends on the stories we dare to tell and the stories we must stop telling. We must tell stories that are as powerful as the truths they're built upon.

So I will keep showing up. As a proud mother. Not always a model minority. As an often-isolated immigrant. A frequently lost—but always searching—multicultural woman. And most of all, as a storyteller. Determined to help build a world where every person and story has a place.

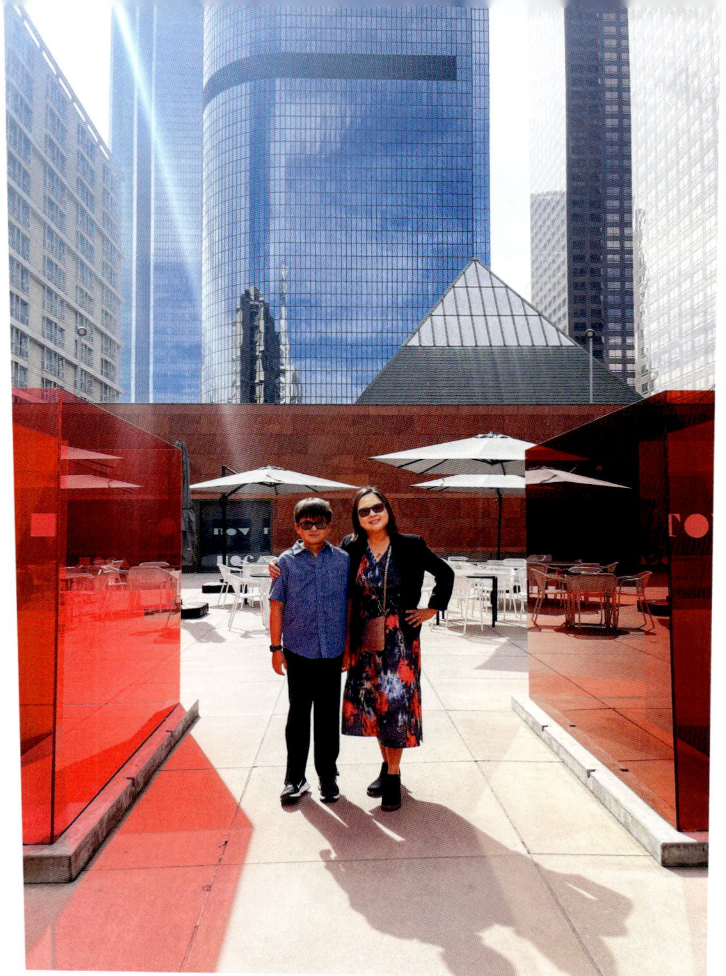

Mother and son at the Museum of Contemporary Art, Grand Ave, Los Angeles. Photo by Foster Kerrison

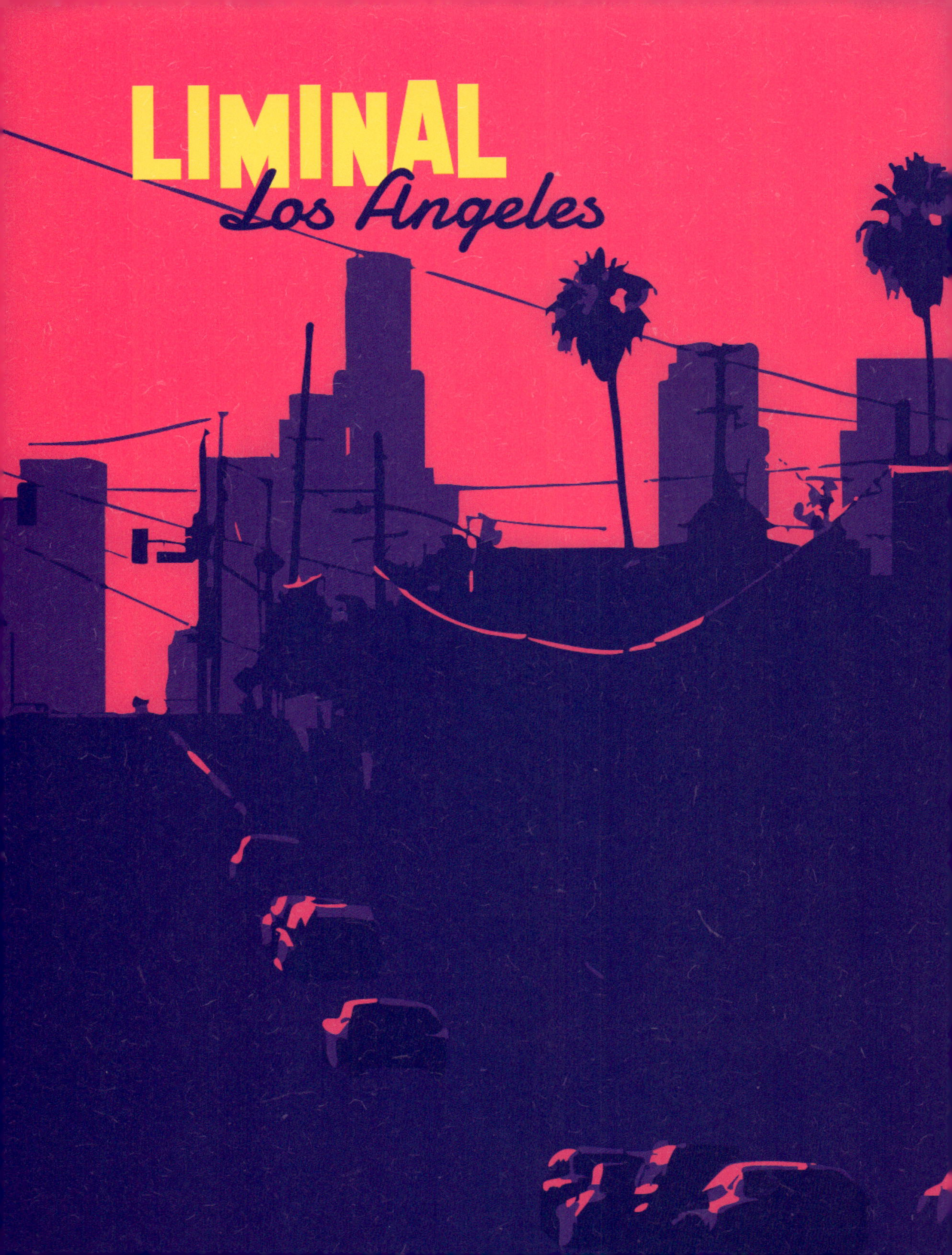
LIMINAL
Los Angeles

In this liminal Los Angeles—a city caught between what was and what could be—I found myself.

For most of my life, I lived in the in-between. I was born Chinese in Surabaya, Indonesia—a minority in a place my family had called home for generations, but where I never felt I truly belonged. On my mother's side, we were *Peranakan*, with deep roots in the archipelago, speaking only Bahasa Indonesia and Javanese. My father's side spoke Cantonese, Mandarin, and Bahasa Indonesia. I spoke a patchwork of all of it: broken Bahasa and Javanese, fragments of Chinese dialects—whatever I could absorb to feel seen, to feel understood.

As the youngest of three, I often felt invisible. I struggled to find my voice because I didn't yet have a language that felt like mine. And just as I was learning to speak one, I had to learn a new one.

When I was three, we relocated to Singapore. There, I attended the Singapore American School where I had to learn English. English quickly became my mother tongue—even though no one else at home spoke it besides my two older siblings. In Singapore, people told me I was too Americanized. In Indonesia, I was no longer Indonesian enough. In their eyes, I was never enough. I lived out of step, out of sync—always slightly misaligned with wherever I found myself.

Then came Boston.

I arrived for college alone, believing—hoping—that America might be the place I could finally belong. But that hope faded quickly. I didn't fit into the Asian American community; I wasn't an American citizen and didn't share their cultural references or histories. I didn't belong in the Singaporean or Indonesian circles either—my American education and accent set me apart. No one claimed me. And at eighteen, that kind of exclusion is quietly devastating.

So I began searching—for others like me. Displaced transplants straddling cultures, suspended between languages, homes, and histories. People who lived in the margins, caught in the constant tension of *unbelonging*. Always slightly adrift. I longed for a kindred spirit—someone who understood what it meant to never fully belong anywhere.

And then I met him.

He was born in Ireland, sent to boarding school at eleven, and by fifteen, had been uprooted again—this time to New Hampshire. Everything familiar had been stripped away. He landed in a country that didn't understand him and didn't want to try. But like me, he endured. We recognized each other immediately—two people unmoored, who had learned to survive by building their own sense of home. For the first time, I didn't feel alone.

We chose to belong to each other.

Now, twenty-five years later, we are married and raising a son together. Our son is mixed-race—full of questions, stories, and wonder. When he cries, "I don't look Chinese. I don't look Irish. I don't belong anywhere!" the ache in his voice is all too familiar. But here, in Los Angeles—a city that welcomes the in-between—we've made a place of belonging for him. He may not look Chinese or Irish, but he looks 100% Californian, American: a home not defined by borders, but by love, memory, and the freedom to be many things at once.

LA didn't ask us to choose. It didn't ask where we were really from or what we were supposed to be. It didn't demand we define ourselves by one language, one identity, one lineage. It was the first place where not belonging felt natural. Most people I meet here have arrived from somewhere else—with a dream, a vision, or simply the hope of beginning again. And the city has made room for that. It thrives in ambiguity. It is a city of shifting narratives and second chances.

Here, I felt something unfamiliar: liberation.

In this "non-place," this ever-evolving urban sprawl of neighborhoods and reinventions, I wasn't an outsider. I was just one of many searching. LA is a city of seekers. A place where you're allowed to not have it all figured out. Where reinvention isn't questioned—it's expected. Where you can become a version of yourself you've never dared to imagine, and the city will nod and say, *Yes, that makes sense here.*

For someone who's lived a life of translation and dislocation, Los Angeles gave me permission to stop explaining. I didn't need to choose a single story. I could hold them all. Or let them go. I could be exactly who I was becoming—and that was enough.

Los Angeles is where I stopped searching for home and realized: I'd been building it all along.

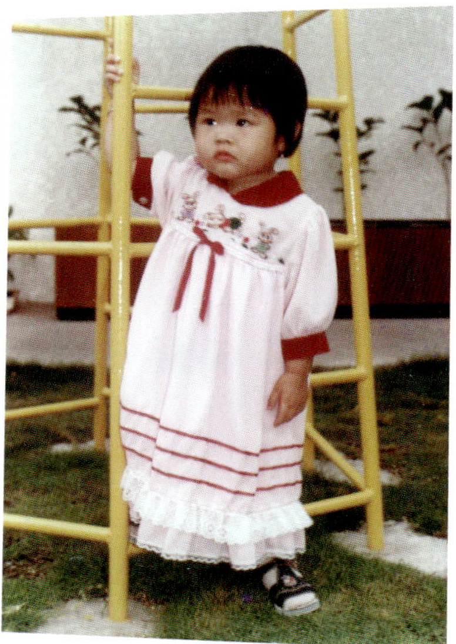

Margaret, two years old,
Surabaya, Indonesia.
Photographer unknown

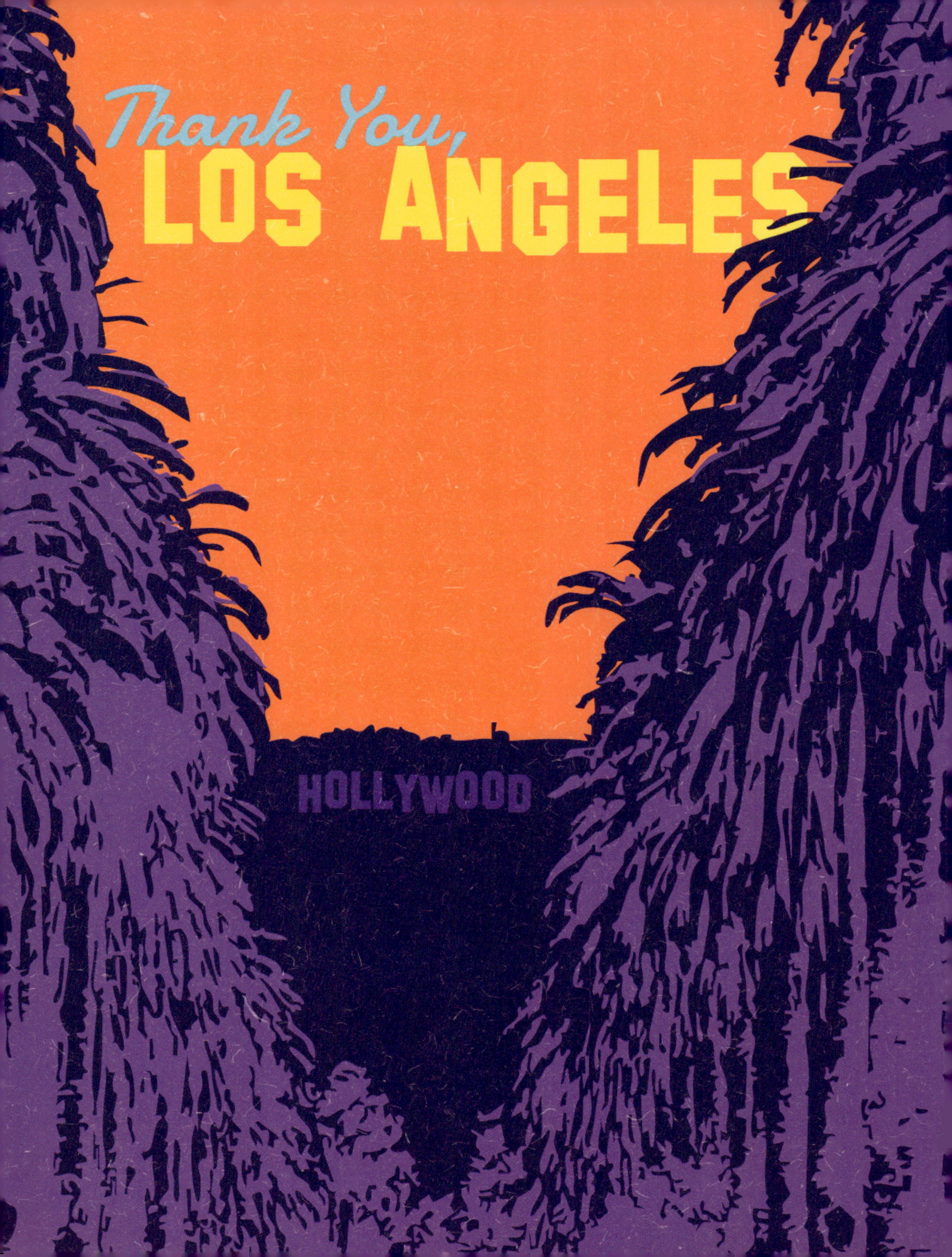
Thank You,
LOS ANGELES
HOLLYWOOD

Like many who came before me, you shaped my story. My journey to you was long—through Indonesia, Singapore, and Boston, across glowing television screens and quiet dreams of a life I had only imagined. But somehow, you were always there, waiting.

You became my window to the world beyond my home. You told stories of adventure and reinvention, offering whispered promises of what could be. Through flickering screens, you showed me a life where children had voices, where people could start over, and where dreams don't just exist within our bedroom walls. You painted a vision of home—one filled with warmth, love, and belonging—even when mine felt far away.

I would sit in my small bedroom in Singapore, drawing, writing, making up stories, while you unfolded before me. On my TV screen, I watched American families gathered around dinner tables, children with chores, allowances, and curfews—people who spoke their minds and were truly heard. I saw backyards filled with green grass, friendships that stood the test of time, and a sense of belonging I deeply yearned for. You were more than entertainment—you were a portal to a world I hoped one day to join.

And finally, I came to you. I finally met you, Los Angeles. The city I had dreamed of, the city that had lived in my mind long before I set foot on your streets.

You dazzled me with your colorful flea markets and neon lights, your show-stopping sunsets and your golden beaches. You overwhelmed me with your vastness, your people, your endless rhythm. Your landscape, a mix of mountains, deserts, and ocean, reflected the diversity of voices that filled your streets. Every corner of you whispered stories—stories of ambition, of struggle, of triumph. You were not just a city; you were a co-creation of narratives, shaped by immigrants like myself, by dreamers, by those who sought something more.

I remember driving through you in a rented van with my family, staring out at your palm-lined streets, your dusty bookstores, your taco stands glowing under the flickering lights of old signs. I remember my first time in Disneyland, stepping onto Main Street and feeling like I had stepped into the very dreams you had promised me. I remember tasting mustard for the first time and deciding, definitively, that it wasn't for me. I remember holding a brown paper bag from a convenience store, pretending I was one of the cool kids I had always seen on TV. Every small moment felt like a piece of a puzzle clicking into place.

You welcomed me, but not in the way I expected. You did not hand me the life I thought I wanted. Instead, you made me search. You made me question. You unraveled the dreams I had borrowed from others and forced me to find my own. I thought I wanted to be a screenwriter, to tell the stories you had once told me. But you showed me that I had my own stories to tell, my own path to carve.

Finding my place in you was not easy. You introduced me to people who became family, to places that became sanctuaries, to challenges that tested my resolve. You did not shield me from your struggles, from your contradictions, from your shadows. You made me understand that to truly belong here, I had to first belong to myself. In your streets, in your markets, in the voices that echoed from Beverly Hills to Koreatown, from Little Tokyo to Pasadena, I saw myself. I heard my own narrative emerging, weaving into the greater tapestry of what makes you, you.

You are more than Rodeo Drive. You are more than Sunset Boulevard. I grew to understand this the longer I stayed. There were pockets of neighborhoods that reflected more of myself. And more of who I wanted to be. I found my people, slowly but surely. Two years wasn't enough to know. Five years gave me a sense. But ten years is really what it took to truly understand and appreciate all the facets of you. A city of paradoxes. A place where the ocean meets the mountains, where wealth and poverty exist side by side, where people from every corner of the world collide and coexist. I found my voice in your cacophony. In the noise, I better heard and knew myself. I found meaning in your contradictions. You are a city of makers, of dreamers, of people who build their own futures from scratch. I am one of them. My story is now one of many, a thread woven into the fabric of this place we all call home.

Your streets are filled with storytellers, and through them, I found my own story. I heard it in the tight-knit community of Leimert Park, in the colorful floats of the Rose Parade, in the mariachi bands of Boyle Heights, in the late-night eats of Koreatown. I felt it in the murals of the

Arts District, in the makeshift signs of family owned thrift stores, in the rhythm of skateboards rolling down Venice Beach's boardwalk. Every voice added to the symphony that is you, Los Angeles. Every story shaped the way I saw myself, the way I learned to belong. And in doing so, I realized that my story, too, had a place here.

You were my teacher, my toughest critic, my complicated love. You gave me the space to explore, to fail, to grow. You taught me that I did not have to be just one thing, that I could be many things. That reinvention was not just a possibility—it was a way of life.

You taught me that identity is fluid, that home is something you build, that belonging is something you create. And now, standing here, I feel more like myself than I ever have before.

Los Angeles, you raised me in ways I never expected. You challenged me, shaped me, and ultimately, embraced me. You did not give me the easy path, but you gave me an honest one. And in doing so, you allowed me to carve out a space that is uniquely mine. No matter where I go, you will always be home. You will always be the place that made me who I am.

Thank you, Los Angeles. *Terima kasih. Xie xie. Kam sia.*

"Wonderful Indonesia" float in the Rose Parade 2013, Pasadena, CA. Photo by Margaret Kerrison

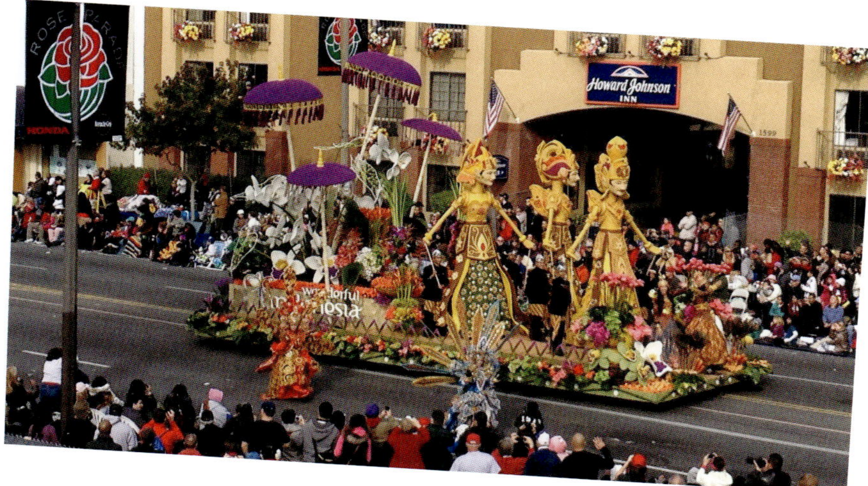

The AMERICA That I Know

As I sit with the final words of this collection, just as I begin to reflect on what it means to belong, yet another tragedy strikes the city I call home. Los Angeles—resilient, radiant, and endlessly complex—now trembles again beneath the weight of injustice.

When you live in a city like Los Angeles, you're always under the world's microscope. People pay attention—because if it can happen here, it can happen anywhere. The world watches in shock and awe: *God, not again. Not Los Angeles.* But it happens here. It always happens here. The chaos and the drama, the beauty and contradiction, all tangled together in this sprawling, radiant city. Because she is a stage—for everyone. This is where the story unfolds. From the Zoot Suit Riots to Watts, from Rodney King to George Floyd, from immigration raids to Hollywood strikes—Los Angeles bears it all. The world watches, because what happens here echoes everywhere. The stage is Los Angeles.

In the heart of Downtown, voices rise in protest. Riots break out in response to aggressive raids led by an administration that sees immigration not as a pillar of this nation, but as a problem to be eradicated. They storm homes with the aim of removing undocumented immigrants—people who have been living quietly, courageously, often invisibly among us. But they are not invisible to me.

They are the ones who braid this city together with strength and dignity. They are the ones who hold us up, who work in the shadows so that the rest of us can live with ease. They care for our children, scrub our schools clean, prepare our meals in kitchens we never see, hammer beams into homes we call safe. They drive our buses, prune our gardens, bag our groceries, and push our society forward without recognition or thanks.

These are not nameless people. They are mothers and fathers, daughters and sons. They are neighbors. They are Angelenos. And their absence—through sudden, violent deportation—tears more than families apart. It shreds the social and moral fabric of our city. My heart breaks.

Each story I hear is not just an individual loss—it's a collective unraveling. Families dismantled in the dead of night. Children coming home to empty houses. Breadwinners gone. Grandparents left behind. And the terrifying silence that follows, echoing with the question: Who will be next?

Unlike so many who live in fear, I was given a path. I came to America legally—as a student, filled with hope and ambition. I studied, I worked hard, and over time, I secured a work sponsor visa. Later, through marriage, I became a citizen. Every step of that process was complex, uncertain, and deeply humbling. I am aware—painfully aware—of my privilege.

It wasn't easy, but it was possible for me. I know, with everything in me, that the same pathway is closed to many others. Closed by bureaucracy. Closed by policy. Closed by prejudice. Closed by financial realities that turn hope into a luxury. And still—they come. Not because it's easy. Not because they're reckless. But because there's hope.

Because there's a dream. A vision of something better. A belief that, despite all its flaws, this country holds a promise that is still worth pursuing.

The America I believe in—the America that opened its doors to me—never asked where I came from. She didn't demand to see my past before she offered me a future. She simply asked what I was willing to give.

And to those who arrive at her doorstep with open hands and hopeful hearts, she says: *Come in*. Brush the dust off your shoes. Bring your story. Bring your struggle. If you're willing to work, to contribute, to grow—then there is space here. There is room for you. There is a life waiting to be built.

She never promised it would be easy. She never said there would be guarantees. But she offered something even more powerful—a chance. A place where you can try, fail, rise again, and try once more. A place where, no matter how crowded or chaotic, there's always room for one more person brave enough to believe. And we believed. With our immigrant roots, we are a family of believers. No one carries belief quite like immigrants do.

My husband came from Ireland, through the quiet suburbs of New Hampshire. I am Chinese-Indonesian, shaped by the multicultural rhythms of Singapore and the winters of Boston. And our son—born in California—is a living, breathing symbol of our shared journey. He carries in him cultures, histories, languages, and a fierce, undeniable Americanness. He is our hope embodied.

It was always my dream to raise my child in America. Not for riches or fame. But for possibility. For the chance to become whoever he wants to be. To walk through the world with confidence and curiosity. To live in a country where identity is not a cage, but a blank canvas. And now—that dream feels threatened.

The country I chose, the one that gave me so much, is changing before my eyes. The values that shaped her—openness, fairness, generosity—are being twisted and rewritten by an administration that governs not with wisdom or care, but with fear and reckless impulse. This is not the America I believed in. This is not the America I love.

But this current administration does not represent all of America. I still believe in the country and city that welcomed me and taught me how to belong—from the people who embraced me as their own. This place gave me more than I ever imagined. I will not surrender its future to fear. I remember my grandmother's words: "Be brave."

I choose to believe. I choose to hope.

To those who seek to tear down what makes this country and city beautiful—you do not speak for me. You do not speak for millions of others who still believe in the core promise of this land.

And yet—even for you—there is space. Because this is America. And in America, we believe in freedom. In free speech, free thought, free will. But that freedom must coexist with respect. With responsibility. With a deep and abiding belief that we are all in this together. Freedom does not mean domination. It does not mean silence for others so your voice can be loudest. It means coexistence. And coexistence demands compassion.

That is the America I know.

And to all who still believe in her—to those who still carry her light—I am with you. I see you. I stand beside you. I will not give up on the promise that brought me here. I will not stop believing in a future that welcomes more hands, more voices, more stories.

We are many. We are different.

We are one people. One city. One nation—still becoming,

still learning how to live up to the promise that built her.

We are all part of her story—no matter what shape we take.

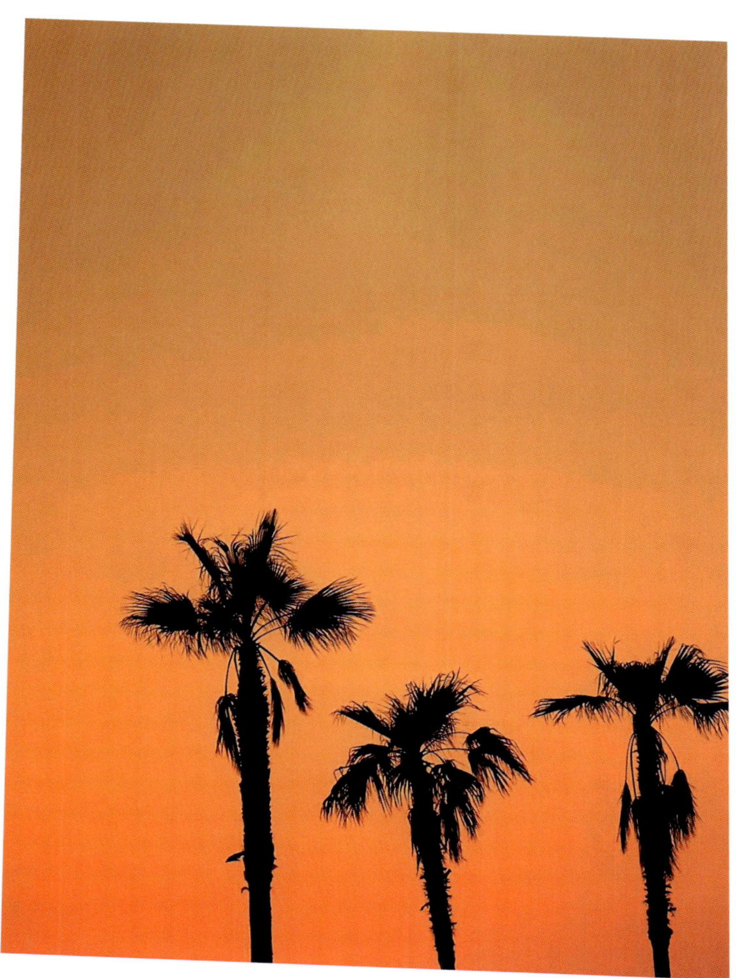

Santa Monica sunset.
Photo by Foster Kerrison

Afterword

Thank you for joining me on this journey. These essays are a collection of my thoughts and observations from the past year, as we all grappled with life-changing events. Faced with the real threat of losing my home and community—and knowing others who did—I found myself deeply reflective, celebrating the place I've called home for over two decades.

This reflection led me on a journey through my memories: from Surabaya, Indonesia, where I was born, to my childhood in Singapore, then immigrating to the United States through Boston, and finally finding my home, identity, and sense of belonging in Los Angeles.

I hope these words resonate with you. Wherever you are—whether in a physical place, a community, or within yourself—I wish for you to find your own place. And more than that, I hope you feel inspired by the possibilities to reinvent and reimagine what your life can be.

Acknowledgments

Thank you to Gordon Goff for giving me yet another opportunity to share my insights and observations with the world. Thank you to Jake Anderson for helping me create this book with such thoughtfulness.

I'm grateful to my friend Josie Huang for writing the heartfelt foreword to my book. I hope you find your new home soon, so you can begin rebuilding your life and creating new shared memories.

Thank you to my husband, Foster, for being my anchor and unwavering support over the years. Your love and patience know no bounds.

Thank you, Bryce, for always reminding me to play, for truly seeing me, and for calling me out when needed. You are my home—my heart in physical form.

Thank you, *Emak*. I know you're watching over me. I miss you every day.

References

Baldwin, Rosecrans. *Everything Now: Lessons from the City-State of Los Angeles.* MCD, 2021.

Baudelaire, Charles. *The Painter of Modern Life and Other Essays.* Translated by Jonathan Mayne, Phaidon Press, 1964.

Benjamin, Walter. *The Arcades Project.* Translated by Howard Eiland and Kevin McLaughlin, Harvard University Press, 1999.

Debord, Guy. "Introduction to a Critique of Urban Geography." 1955.

de Botton, Alain. "A Good Idea from Charles Baudelaire." *US Modernist*, 2006.

de Botton, Alain, and John Armstrong. *Art as Therapy*. Phaidon Press, 2013.

Eames, Charles and Ray. Various works and design philosophy. [General reference to their creative practice and collaboration.]

Elkin, Lauren. *Flâneuse: Women Walk the City in Paris, New York, Tokyo, Venice, and London*. Vintage, 2017.

Hall, Edward T. *The Hidden Dimension*. Anchor Books, 1966.

Hopper, Edward. *Nighthawks* (1942) and *Automat* (1927). The Art Institute of Chicago and Philadelphia Museum of Art.

Jacobs, Jane. *The Death and Life of Great American Cities*. Random House, 1961.

Kerrison, Margaret. *Immersive Storytelling for Real and Imagined Worlds*. Michael Wiese Productions, 2022.

Kerrison, Margaret. *Reimagined Worlds: Narrative Placemaking for People, Play, and Purpose*. ORO Editions, 2024.

Kerrison, Margaret. *The Art of Immersive Storytelling: Strategies from the Gaming World*. Michael Wiese Productions, 2025.

Lou, Liza. *Kitchen*. Whitney Museum of American Art, New York.

McCue, Frances. "Flâneur: City Wanderer." *US Modernist*, 2006.

McMillen, Michael C. *Central Meridian (The Garage)*. Los Angeles County Museum of Art.

Oldenburg, Ray. *The Great Good Place*. Marlowe & Company, 1989.

Solnit, Rebecca. *A Field Guide to Getting Lost*. Viking, 2005.

Solnit, Rebecca. *Wanderlust: A History of Walking*. Viking, 2000.

Speck, Jeff. *Walkable City: How Downtown Can Save America, One Step at a Time*. Farrar, Straus and Giroux, 2012.

Suh, Do Ho. Various installation works. [General reference to artist's creative practice.]

About the Author

Born in Indonesia and raised in Singapore, Margaret's career spans over seventeen years of creating narratives and writing for television, film, digital media, games, brand storytelling, location-based entertainment, narrative placemaking, and immersive experiences. As a writer–creative director, she has designed experiences for some of the most beloved brands in the world and has worked on project teams that have won six Thea Awards from the Themed Entertainment Association. She is the author of *Immersive Storytelling for Real and Imagined Worlds* (MWP, 2022), *Reimagined Worlds: Narrative Placemaking for People, Play, and Purpose* (ORO Editions, 2024), and *The Art of Immersive Storytelling: Strategies from the Gaming World* (MWP, 2025). In 2023, she was awarded the prestigious Paul Helmle Fellowship by the Department of Architecture at California Polytechnic State University, Pomona. She lives in Los Angeles with her husband and son and is always looking for her next adventure and invitation to play.

HTTPS://MARGARETKERRISON.MY.CANVA.SITE

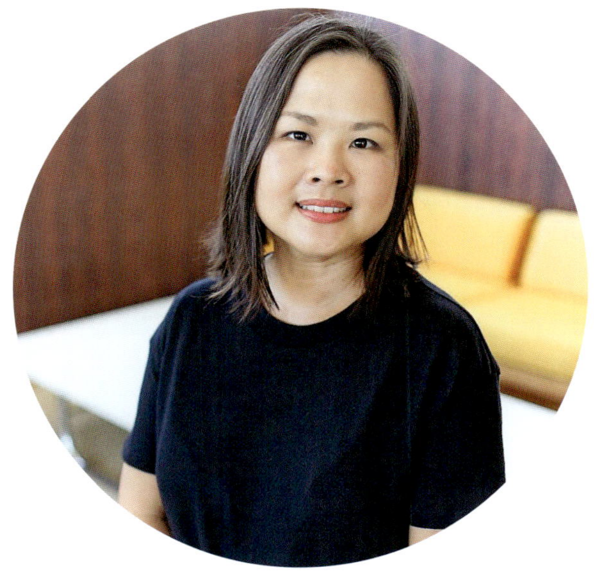

immersivestory2022@gmail.com

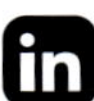

www.linkedin.com/in/margaret-chandra-kerrison-1840817

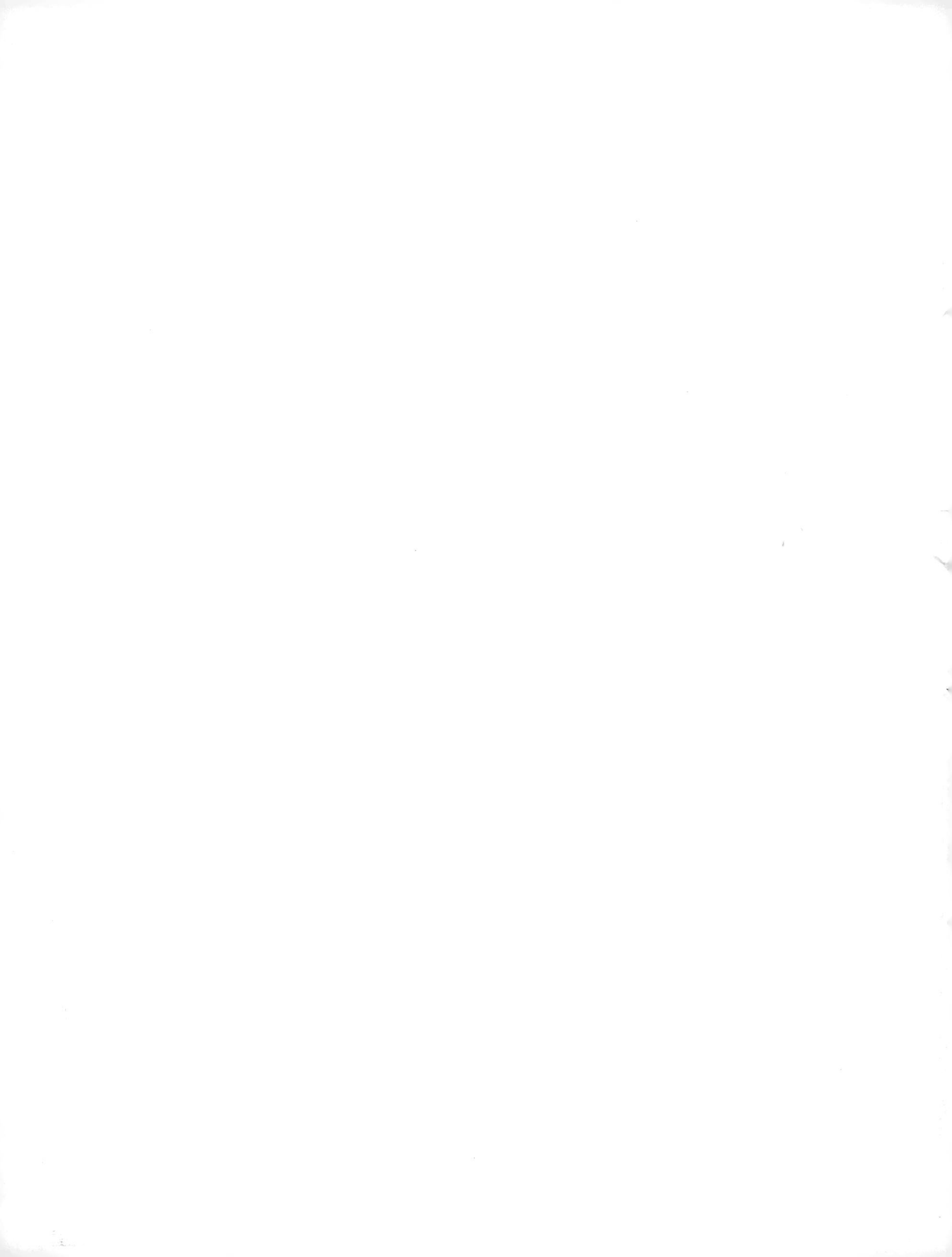